Janet O'Hare   FOD

Taunton

An A-Z

Taunton

An A-Z

Lionel Ward

L E Ward

Onyx Publishing

2008

Published by
Onyx Publishing
Brendon Books
Old Brewery Buildings
Bath Place
Taunton
TA1 4ER

01823 337742

ISBN 0-9532876-2-9
978-0-9532876-2-8

Printed and bound in Great Britain by
TJ International Ltd
Trecerus Industrial Estate
Padstow
Cornwall PL28 8RW

Acknowledgements

David Bromwich, and all other staff at the Local Studies Library in Taunton who helped me, and the Somerset Record Office. As a bookseller of 20 years in Taunton I am also lucky enough to have available to me a wide variety of sources from our current stock of books and from publications I have collected over the years.

Most of the illustrations are my own photographs or from sources specified as being in the public domain, either because copyright has expired or they have voluntarily been placed in the public domain. For several of the illustrations, I would like to thank the The Somerset Archaeological and Natural History Society (marked as SANHS), The Mayors Office for the picture of the first Mayor and the top of the Mace, and to Clare Bennett for the pictures of the flood in Bridge Street and of a picture by Francis Colthurst. There are a few occasions where I have not been able to identify or contact the source.

A particularly big thank you to my wife Jo for her editing skills, which were in great demand.

To Jo

Alleine, Joseph (1633-1668)

An influential theologian who was Vicar George Newton's assistant at St Mary Magdalene in Taunton. Some of his work remains in print to this day.

Born at Devizes, Wiltshire. When his older brother died while studying for the ministry, he pleaded with his father to take his place, undergoing what he described as a 'thorough conversion'. He entered Oxford at 16. Graduating in 1653, he worked as a college tutor and then as a Chaplain, turning down a fellowship at Corpus Christi College and refusing high offices of preferment.

He did, however, accept an invitation to become Vicar George Newton's assistant at St Mary Magdalene in Taunton in 1655. He also married about this time his cousin, Theodosia Alleine, daughter of Richard Alleine, minister of Batcombe in Somerset.

A

CALL

TO

THE UNCONVERTED

TO WHICH ARE ADDED,

SEVERAL VALUABLE ESSAYS.

In addition to his theological studies he was fascinated with scientific research and would work through the night conducting experiments. He also wrote a book in which he attempted to show that religion and science went hand in hand. Unfortunately, this manuscript was lost. His influential treatise, 'An Alarm to the Un-converted', however (also published as 'A Sure Guide to Heaven'), still remains in print. 'Your sins will not die with you,' he claims, 'they will go to hell with you there to be your tormentors.' He argued that Christ can save you for 'Does he not keep the keys of heaven and can you not go in without his leave?'

'If I should die 50 miles away, let me be buried in Taunton.'

Both Alleine and Vicar George Newton were ejected from their posts at St Mary's in 1662 for their dissenting views. He became a wandering preacher, preaching wherever the opportunity arose. On the 26 May 1663 he was committed to Ilchester Gaol for preaching at a service the previous week.

The conventicle of the following year stated that no more than five people were allowed in a religious assembly outside of the established church. Alleine, though, continued to preach on his release from prison on 20 May 1664. The imposition of the Five Mile Act of 1665 made his situation even more difficult. The act prohibited any dissenting minister to preach within five miles of where he had formerly preached unless he took an oath to support the king and swore never to attempt to alter the government of church or state, something that Alleine felt he could not do. After accepting the hospitality of the merchant John Mallack at Fullands just outside the centre of the town, he became ill. He decided that he would make his way to his home town of Devizes to 'take the waters', but before he could do so, on the 10 July 1665, he was arrested once more, for preaching at Fullands. After suffering further persecution and re-leased from prison, he returned to Taunton in February 1668 where he became very ill. He died on the 17 November 1668, aged 34. A grave was eventually found for him at St Mary Magdalene's Church.

He said during his lifetime, 'If I die fifty miles away, let me be buried in Taunton.' He was also quoted as saying, 'The Vineyard of the hosts is the town of Taunton and the inhabitants thereof his precious plant.'

Alma Street

Named after the battle of Alma (20 September 1854) which took place near the River Alma in the Ukraine, the first battle of the Crimean War.

A British and French force un-der Lord Raglan and General St Arnaud and a smaller Turkish contingent defeated a Russian army under General Menshikov.

They dislodged the Russians from their position on the heights above the Alma River. The Russians lost nearly 6,000 men and the British 2,000. The French claimed they lost 1,300, though Lord Raglan claimed it was nearer 500.

The victory was so popular at home that it became a popular name for girls and public houses as well as for a number of streets.

A 'Broadside' ballad was also brought out entitled 'The Battle of Alma'. It began:

> *You Loyal Britains pray draw near*
> *Unto the news I've brought you here*
> *With Joy each British heart does cheer*
> *For the victory gained at Alma*

Almshouses

Charitable housing for the elderly which is still in evidence in
Taunton today.

Gray's Almshouses in East Street in Taunton are still in use today. They were founded by Robert Gray, a successful London businessman born in Taunton. The inscription on the stone at the front of the building reads:

> *'Laus Deo. This charitable work is founded by Robert Graye, of the cittie of London, esquire, borne in this towne, in the house adjoining here unto, who in his life-time doth erect it for tenn poore aged single women: and for their competent liveli-hood, and daylie prayers in the same, provided maintenance for the same. 1635.'*

However, on a tablet in the church dated 1751 it is stated that the almshouses were for 'six poor men and a reader, and ten poor women', indicating that the almshouses were improved and extended.

Though he had already selected his trustees, Robert Gray died before his will was completed though he had already purchased the land and built a chapel and 'the apartments for the woman and the reader.' The Mayor of the time, though, Robert Moggridge, successfully applied to have his wishes carried out and £2,000 was made available from his will to the trustees, 'for the purpose of purchasing lands, the net rent of which, and in the mean time the interest of the money, was wholly to be applied to the support of the foundation.'

There were additional donations and legacies bequeathed to Gray's Almshouses over the years. In 1754 John Noble gave £500, 'afterwards secured on the tolls of Taunton market.', and in 1772 John Coles gave £300, 'afterwards secured on the tolls of the Taunton turnpikes.'

The administration of the almshouses passed from the Trustees of Gray's Almshouses to the Trustees of Taunton Town Charity in the 1960's. They were refurbished and modernised in 1989 and now provide sheltered accommodation.

Gray's Almshouses in East Reach, still in use today.

Huish's Almshouses. Richard Huish founded almshouses on the north side of Hammet Street. They were described by Toulmin in his History of Taunton as 'a large good house'. From end to end they were about 95 feet long, 'laid out in into a chapel and thirteen seperate rooms, for thirteen poor, needy, maimed, impotent, or aged men, who have been of honest frame and good report.', and were administered by 22 governors, 'who must be resident in Taunton or within twelve miles of it.' After his death, Huish's property, the source of the money for the almshouses, was destroyed by the great fire of London in 1666. However, the situation was restored by an act of chancery in December 1672. After a later period of neglect, by a decree of chancery of 21 June 1735, new governors were appointed and the endowment re-established.

Richard Huish in his will of 1615 left money for the etsablishment of a hospital for 24 'elderly poor men' and five scholarships to Oxford and Cambridge. Some of the money from the endowment was subsequnetly used to help fund Richard Huish's Secondary School and Bishop Fox's School for Girls.

St Margaret's Almshouses. Situated in Hamilton Road and dating from the 12th century, this was originally a leper hospital. In the early 16th century, Glastonbury Abbey, who had acquired the patronage of the hospital under Abbot Bere, rebuilt the building as almshouses. With the dissolution of the monasteries the accompanying chapel was sold. It was demolished in 1930. The building continued to be used as an almshouse until it became the head-

Former leper hospital and Almshouse in Hamilton Road

quarters of the Somerset Guild of Master Craftsmen and Rural Community Council in 1938. After their move to new premises at the end of the 1980's, it remained empty for some time suffering vandalism and a fire before being taken over by the Somerset Building Preservation Trust who, in association with the Falcon Rural Housing Association, repaired the building to create four cottages.

Henley's Almshouses. These were situated at the west end of St Mary's Church. They were founded by Dorothy Henley in 1637 and comprised 18 rooms. By 1788 they were reported as being in a 'ruinous state' and 'a public nuisance.' It was estimated that the almshouses would cost £100 to repair. Benjamin Hammett intervened and built some new almshouses in Holway Lane (now South Street) bearing the name of Henley's Almshouses.

Pope's Almshouses. These were to the east of Gray's Almshouses consisting of 14 rooms, though the exact date of their inception is unknown. According to hearsay, when Toulmin was writing in the late eighteenth century, it was the gift of Mrs Grace Portman. They were damaged by fire in the Civil War and rebuilt by a man named Pope from which they took their name. They were demolished in 1933 and the proceeds put towards building Leycroft Almshouses for 29 people in Hamilton Road.

St James Street Almshouses. The site of these almshouses belonged to the Priory. There is reference to buildings in 1545, though no reference to them as almshouses until 1821. They needed £500 for repair in 1869. The site was sold to Hanbury and Cotchin, the Canon Street Brewery and it is believed that they were taken down in about 1897. Two of the best timber frames were re-created in the Castle moat until they eventually deteriorated to such a degree that a decision was made to reconstruct one of the dwellings with walls and interior features within the Castle courtyard.

Alsmhouses at St James's Close still in use today.

Almshouses, still in use today, were opened in St James's Close in 1845 in the shadow of St James's Church. They were renovated in 1968 and contain 10 one bed flats

Magdalene Lane Almshouses. In the parish records there is reference to 'seventeen houses in Little Magdalene Lane, and two in St Paul's Street.' These are thought to have been built by Thomas Osborne in 1435, originally to house seven tenements. They were reconstructed in 1845 and closed in 1932.

Amory, Dr Thomas (1701-1774)

Born in Taunton, he was the son of a grocer, John and Anne, the sister of Henry Grove (who became the head of the Taunton Dissenting Academy).

Amory entered the Academy on 25 March 1717 and then went to study under Reverend John Eames at Moorfields in London. He returned to Taunton to help with teaching at the Academy and between 1725 and 1730 became the assistant to Robert Darch at Bishop's Hull Church. He then became the assistant to Edmund Batson, who was in poor health, at St Paul's Meeting House. However there was disagreement between Batson and Amory, whose views were more liberal, and Batson refused to share his income with Amory. A vocal minority supported Amory. He resigned in 1732 and went to a new meeting house in Tancred Street. In 1738, following the death of Henry Grove, he became head of the Taunton Academy. He married, the daughter of a London minister and in 1759 he moved to London to preach at the Old Jewery and to agitate for church reform. He died on 24 June 1774.

In 1724 he wrote the following poem about his native Taunton.

Taunton

Hail! Native town with cheerful plenty bless'd,
Of numerous hands and thriving trade possess'd:
Whose poor might live from biting want secure,
Did not resist less ale their hearts allure.
Round thee in spring, we view with ravish'd eyes,
Italian scenes in English ground arise;
Which, crown'd with freedom, rival paradise,
Th'enammell'd meads with vast profusion show
The various colours of the heavenly bow,

The fat'ning Tone in slow meander moves,
Loath to forsake the happy land it loves
Forc'd to the main, by nature's law, it bears,
Back floating vessels fraught with richest wares;
And differing products from earth's differing shores,
Gather'd by commerce, lavish, on us pours.
Upon its borders herds unnumbered graze,
With sheep whose fleeces Persian silks surpass;
nor prowling wolves, nor hungry lions fear.
With other flocks, in other pastures tear.
Tall bushy trees. O'er all the region found,
With cooling shades refresh the fertile ground;
Beneath whose coverts beauteous females stray,
Fresh, artless, gentle, innocently gay.
And pass, with faltering swains, the sportful hours away,
Sighing they listen to the amorous tale,
Nor fear lest wily snakes their steps assail.
Gay, painted blossoms smile on lower trees,
With promis'd nectar thirsty palates please,
And with their sweets perfume the vernal breeze.
While warbling birds melodious notes employ,
At once exalt , and tell, the shepherd's joy,
Here fruitful hillocks swell amidst the plain,
In verdue clad, and rich in future grain;
Adown whose sides the murm'ring torrents roll,
And charm the muse to bless the poets soul.
And all around proud guardian hill ascend,
Whose height from winds inclement well defend;
Whose bowls unknown stories of minerals hold,
Which poverty disarm, and chase th'invading cold.
But I unequal, tempt the arduous toil:
Large as they vales, and generous as thy soil,
The verse should be, which would they praise proclaim,
In numbers worthy of the matchless theme.

Bath Place

Bath Place is one of Taunton's oldest thoroughfares and may have been the main route west from Taunton in the middle ages.

No other name than footway appears until the end of the eighteenth century when the name Hunt's Court appears. It may have been named after Hugh Hunt who owned property in the area.

Bath Place was bought by Sir Benjamin Hammett in 1791 and it is thought that his son was responsible for the construction of the terrace buildings on the south side which comprise the shops of today. They are first shown on a map of the town dated 1849. It is also about this time we see the first use of the name Bath Place rather than Hunt's Court.

According to Goldsworthy writing in 1883, Bath Place in the 1800's was 'a rough and dirty court'. There was an open drain next to the archway 'where all the abominations from the courts in the High Street and the Crescent Houses were soon passing down.' Among its occupants were several sedan carriers, 'The Holes, Houses and Priddys: Billy Upham, the postman, two bakers and a greengrocer: Sally Allen, a laundress, and Phil Rodber, the surgeon.'

Goldsworthy accepted that Bath Place had been widened and improved at the time of his writing though he also stated that 'there is no part of the town where greater improvements are needed.'

The courtyard at the eastern end of Bath Place

A Quaker Meeting House was built in 1693 just beyond the 'tunnel' at the West End of Bath Place where the town gates were positioned. It was often a requirement that non-conformist places of worship should be positioned outside the town walls. A new building was built at the same site in 1814.

A Public Hall was built by William Beadon of Otterford at the High Street end of Bath Place, provided Member of Parliament, E. T. Bainbridge. The Mechanics Institute moved there from Paul Street in the early 1840's to be succeeded by the School of Art in 1856. It remained there until 1889. This was the precursor of the Somerset College of Arts and Technology.

Commemorative plaque in Bath Place

Charles G Webb established a printing press in Bath Place producing Webb's Weekly Advertising News in May 1868 & the Standard of Freedom in October 1868. This became absorbed by the Taunton Sun which began publication in April 1875. In 1874 he reprinted Savage's edition of Toulmin's History of Taunton there.

Harry Frier, the noted local painter (see seperate entry) was a resident of Bath Place between 1895 and 1897.

Bath Place today is an interesting mix of independent retailers and domestic dwellings.

Bear Baiting & Bull Baiting

Bear baiting was a popular pastime in Elizabethan times. A particular incident relating to Taunton is recorded in the proceedings of the Star Chamber of the Palace of Westminster in 1592. A notorious gang called the 'Horner Gang' had been terrorising Taunton and at about midnight, armed with weapons, approached George Webb, who was a bearkeeper in Taunton, and demanded that he bring his bear out to be baited in the market square. When he refused, they broke in and took the bear out into the streets of the town and beyond, 'hollowing and making strange outcrys and unwanted noyses,

beating at the door of divers people; and some of the said doors did they broke open, and suffered the sayd Beare to rome about loose, there by disturbing the whole Town....whereby many of the inhabitants were so terrified that they were like to have been dryven out of their wittes and fallen madd.' The bear was then taken into the market square and baited, 'and did hurt very dangerously sundry of the inhabitants of the said Town which had in courteous manner endeavoured to persuade them to surcease and leave of their said demeanours.'

Bull baiting was tolerated not just as a sport but because it was thought that a bull that was baited provided better quality meat. In the 17th century in the market in Taunton a rope and collar was provided for this very purpose. However, in the 19th century, there were moves to ban it. The following is from the Dorchester, Sherborne and Taunton Journal of 21 June, 1821:

'The often, but vainly denounced practice of bull-baiting presented another of its shocking exhibitions on Monday last at Rumwell, near Taunton, where a bull was in the afternoon taken to the stake and bound, but it appears not securely enough for the intentions of his persecutors, for having endured the savage ferocity of the dogs, and their no less savage masters, for some time, he broke loose and gored and tossed some of the bystanders in so serious a way that we have heard that they will have reason to recollect a bull-bait for the rest of their lives. Not satisfied, the followers of this sport afterwards succeeded in leading the poor animal to the scene of his torture two or three times in succession, whence on each occasion, he escaped, causing considerable mischief to eight or nine individuals, and to one young man in particular, a recruit, who had his legs most severely broken and splintered.'

Though a bill was presented to parliament in 1802 it was defeated by 13 votes and was not outlawed until the passing of the Cruelty to Animals Act of 1835.

Cock-fighting, was a popular pastime in Taunton, played at a variety of places, and could be a major event. The Western Flying Post of 18 February 1771 such advertised an event at the White Hart Inn. The details were as follows:

'A main of thirty-one cocks of each side and to fight the two following days, for four guineas a Battle, and Twenty the odd Battle, between the gentlemen of the eastern part of Somerset, and the Gentleman of the western part.'

Goldsworthy in his Recollections of Taunton describes how game cocks were bred especially for fighting. 'After the battle, they were taken up lame, bleeding and nearly feather less, with heads pecked raw and eyes knocked out; sometimes they were picked up dead, having had a steel spur knocked into their brains.' He continues, 'I have often seen my brother preparing his cocks for battle by giving them stimulating food, buckling spurs on their heels, and crowing like a cock; and, after the battle, bathing their heads with milk and water.'

Other cruel sports which were still in existence in the early nineteenth century included Badger-drawing, where a badger was put into a barrel and dogs were encouraged to pull him out (according to Goldsworthy, 'as cruel a business as could be devised.'), and fights between bulldogs where 'The victor and vanquished generally left the ground limping, maimed, and sadly mutilated.'

Bishop Fox's, Richard Huish & King's College Schools

The three schools, King's College, Richard Huish College and Bishop Fox's School share an intertwined history. King's College was the site for the original grammar school which had been based in the Old Municipal Buildings in Corporation Street. Though it closed after its return to the Municipal Buildings, it had its bequest transferred to Bishop Fox's School while both the Richard Huish College and Bishop Fox's School enjoyed a common bequest from the Huish endowment.

In 1522 Bishop Richard Fox of Winchester is thought to have been responsible for the establishment of a grammar school in what now forms the eastern part of the Municipal Buildings in Corporation Street. The school closed through shortage of funds after Richard Fox's death but was reopened with money from the

Bishop Richard Fox, Bishop of Winchester 1501 - 1528.
His motto was Est Deo Gratia (Thanks Be To God).

merchant, Roger Hill, from about 1533, until his death in about 1545. It did not reopen until money was forthcoming from William Walby of Corpus Christi, Oxford in 1554. It appears that the school continued in a modest way until in 1864, the Reverend William Tuckwell was appointed and helped increase the size of the school and the quality of the education.

A new school was planned on 15 acres of land purchased for £3,000 at the site of the old racecourse off South Road. Lord Taunton (Henry Labouchere), headed a company which built the new school. A contract was signed with John Spiller of Bridge Street for £11,285. The school took two years to build and was opened in April 1870. Unfortunately, Lord Taunton did not see the opening of the school as he died the year before at Quantock Lodge, his family home. Reverend Tuckwell, no doubt, felt the loss of his influence when events and some of the local clergy conspired against him. There were two outbreaks of scarlet fever and there was criticism of his teaching which emphasised science, not considered a suitable subject by many of the local clergy at that time. The number of pupils declined and Tuckwell resigned in September 1877. The school closed down in July 1879 and returned to its original site at the Municipal Buildings under the new headmaster, Henry Knapton, until it was closed in 1885.

The school in South Road was acquired by Canon Woodard for £8,000 after it failed to sell at auction. Woodard preached the value of education as a mainstay to public order and propounded the need for less expensive schools for the emerging middle classes who could not afford the established public schools. He also saw an opportunity for the established church to be influential in education.

Funds were raised with difficulty but the school eventually opened in October 1880. It was christened King Alfred's School after King Alfred unlike other Woodard schools which took the names of saints.

Numbers grew from 9 in the first year to 68 in 1883. However, after this good start, numbers declined, in part due to further outbreaks of scarlet fever and in part to lack of good support for the headmaster, Rev. Thompson. By

King's College

1896 the school only had 21 pupils and the school closed for a year. Under the new headmaster, Rev. Edward Boswell Vincent, numbers increased to 120 within five years.

In 1944 Gatcombe, a large private house was purchased, and Fullands House (formerly a mental institution, then a school in its own right before reverting to a private residence). After the war Pyrland Hall was bought for £10,000 and became a junior school, King's Hall.

When the Grammar School had vacated the Municipal Buildings in 1870, an independent 'middle-class school' took its place. It was established by Reverend H. G. Rogers, son of the founder of Fulland's School (1840 -1888). It began receiving surplus funds from Richard Huish's charity and from 1874 it became known as Huish's Middle-class School. It had to move to temporary buildings when the Grammar School returned in 1880. The following year, however, the Huish School moved to the site of Green's Commercial School in East Street where it was able to expand with the help of grants from the County Council, until it moved to South

The current Bishop Fox's School in Calway Road

Road in 1964. In 1979 it became a sixth form college.

Meanwhile, the Huish charity also contributed to the founding of a girl's school in the Crescent at the current site of the Masonic Hall, The Huish School for Girls. The first headmistress was Miss Emily Reeves. The bequest of William Walby which had originally been used to help fund the first grammar school, now that it was closed, was transferred to the girls school in 1890 along with an endowment of William Poole (from 30 acres of land at Hawkchurch and £100 from the Taunton Town Charities). In 1895 the endowment scheme was further extended and grants were awarded by the local authority enabling a school to be built at a new site in Staplegrove Road at the site of the The Laurel's Nurseries. The school opened in 1905 as Bishop Fox's School for Girls. A new science wing and classroom was added in 1907.

In 1940 it moved again to a site on Kingston Road. It became a girl's comprehensive in 1978 and a mixed comprehensive in 1980. In 1994 it moved yet again to a new site off Calway Road, fittingly behind Richard Huish College and only a short distance from King's College. The school received an award from the Royal Society of Arts for the quality of the architecture. The current Bishop Fox's School can, therefore, claim by a circuitous route, a link with the original foundation of the grammar school established in the early 16th century.

Robert Blake (1599-1657)

Though born in Bridgwater he is remembered in Taunton for his dogged defence of Taunton against the Royalists during the Civil War.

The eldest of eight children in 1615 he went to Wadham College Oxford where he is thought to have developed his strong republican principles. He returned to Bridgwater in 1625 on the death of his father to take over the family business.

He was elected an MP for Bridgwater under the Short Parliament in 1640.

Commanding a company during the first civil war (1642-1646) he was criticised for defending Prior's Hill fort after Colonel Fiennes had already surrendered to Prince Rupert in July 1643. As lieutenant-colonel he led an unsuccessful surprise attack on Bridgwater in which his brother was killed, before moving to Lyme Regis where the garrison was besieged by Prince Maurice (Prince Rupert's brother) in April 1644. He was able to defend the town, shipping in supplies and reinforcements by sea, until he was relieved by the Earl of Essex two months later. It was this last action that secured his promotion to Colonel. He then marched all the way to Taunton, took the town and survived repeated attempts by the Royalists to siege the town before being relieved by Sir Thomas Fairfax in May 1645. He famously declared that he had four pairs of boots and would eat three before he

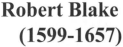

> Blake declared that he had four pairs of boots and would eat three pairs before he would surrender Taunton

would surrender Taunton. He then went on to Dunster Castle which he seized in April 1646. That same year he was elected MP for Bridgwater.

Though we mainly remember Blake for his activities during the Civil War, to many his exploits at sea are at least as important. He is considered second only to Nelson in stature in British naval history.

Blake was appointed one of the commissioners of the navy and set sail against Prince Rupert at Kinsale (Southern Ireland) in May 1649. He chased him to Portugal and seized his Brazilian plunder, in effect forcing Portugal and Spain to recognise the English Commonwealth.

In 1651 he captured a Royalist base on the Isle of Scilly and a stronghold at Jersey.

When the Anglo-Dutch war broke out in 1652 he saw off a fleet of twelve ships under the command of Admiral Maarten Tromp near Dover and a fleet commanded by Vice-Admiral de Witte before being defeated by Tromp at Dungeness at the end of November 1652.

His resignation was refused by the government who instead preferred to review naval tactics. In a further engagement with Tromp in February 1653 off Portland, with a refitted fleet, he was triumphant and he was instrumental in later victory over Tromp at North Foreland (in June). However, as a result of these campaigns he did suffer a leg injury from which he never completely recovered and he was not well enough to take part in the final Anglo-Dutch War at Scheveningen in July 1653, when Tromp was killed.

Blake's next adventure was in the Mediterranean in October 1654 where he successfully destroyed the shore batteries at Porto Farina (Tunisia) and the fleet of the Barbary pirates who had been preying on English shipping.

During the Anglo-Spanish Civil War in March 1656 he set sail from Portsmouth and blockaded the port of Cadiz enabling Captain Richard Stayner to capture booty from Spanish ships returning from the West Indies.

His greatest victory, though, was in April 1857 at Santa Cruz when he destroyed a fleet of Spanish ships who were docked in the harbour without losing a single English ship.

He died within sight of Plymouth harbour on 7 August 1657 aboard his flagship, *The George*. He received a state funeral.

Buffalo Bill

The legendary Col. W. F. Cody, 'Buffalo Bill', came to town on bank holiday Monday 1 August 1903. The show which took place at the Poor Grounds, East Reach, was eagerly anticipated.

The Somerset County Herald of 8th August reported the event.

BANK HOLIDAY
TAUNTON, MONDAY, AUGUST 3rd.
LOCATION—POOR GROUNDS.

BUFFALO BILL'S WILD WEST
AND
Congress of Rough Riders of the World.
Headed and Personally Introduced by
Col. W. F. CODY, "BUFFALO BILL."
Now Touring the Provinces on its own Special Trains, Visiting the
Principal Cities and Greater Railway Centres Only.
FOUR SPECIAL TRAINS. 800 PEOPLE. 500 HORSES.
A Proudly Pre-eminent Exhibition of Universal Interest.

The One Grand Ruler of the Amusement Realm
Standing like an obelisk above and beyond all others.

LIVING OBJECT LESSONS
Taken from the pages of realism, and illustrated by the very men who have assisted in making the fame of the

Mounted Warriors of the World,
A Gathering of extraordinary consequence to fittingly depict all that
Virile, Muscular, Heroic
Manhood
Has and can endure.
The Veteran Cavalry of many Flags
In Military Evolutions and Exercises.
Royal English Lancers,
Bedouin Arabs,
South American Gauchos,
United States Cavalry,
Cuban Patriots,
Russian Cossacks,
Roosevelt Rough Riders,
American Artillery,
Mexican Ruralles,
Realistic Military Spectacles
The Battle of San Juan Hill

TWICE DAILY, RAIN OR SHINE.

Typical Cow-Boys of the Western Plains, Wild West Girls, Scouts, and Crackshots.

The Vast Arena Illuminated at Night by Two Special Electric Light Plants.

TWO PERFORMANCES EVERY WEEK DAY,

'Not within living memory has there been such a crowd in one day at Taunton. From early morning up to noon excursion trains were bringing young, old and middle aged from the whole of Somerset, and also from the principle towns of the adjoining counties, while even some of the residents of South Wales put in an appearance. It is a unique exhibition - for their is only one Wild West Show - and once seen it can never be forgotten for its picturesqueness, the healthy excitement it creates, and the general dash of the whole business. It is estimated that the afternoon show was visited by fully fourteen thousand people, who had the pleasure of seeing the magnificent combination. The program in all consisted in over twenty items. The opening portion was a grand revue of the rough riders of the world, led by Colonel Cody.' This was followed by 'exhibitions of feats in the saddle', a recreation of the attack on the Deadwood Mail Coach, and then 'Colonel Cody exhibits his deadly prowess as a shot by shattering glass balls, thrown up in the air, even when the horse is at full pace'. There was also 'a clever acrobatic of play, a Red Indian war dance ..... and the illustrations of the battle of Sean Jean Hill. Altogether the programme was a very delightful and enjoyable one and Colonel Cody and his performers at the close came in for a good outburst of applause.'

Camden, William (1551 - 1623)

An usher of Westminster School, during the school vacations he travelled throughout the country recording what he saw. He began Britannia, a description of each county of Britain in 1577.

The first Edition of Britannia was published in Latin in 1586. By 1607 it had reached its seventh edition. In it he attempted to show how the past could be discerned from the existing landscape. It is considered one of the great works of 16th century scholarship. The following extract on Taunton was taken from a translation by Philemon Holland:

'....*Thone runneth by Thonton, commonly Taunton, and giveth its name. A verie fine and proper towne this is indeed, and most pleasantly seated: in a word, one of the eieis of this shire, where Ina King of the West Saxons built a castle which Desburgia his wife raced and laid even with the ground after she had expelled from thence Eadbritch King of the South Saxons, who now mad himself a Lord thereof, and used it as a bridle to keepe the countrey under that he had subdued. When Edward the Confessour was King, it paid tribute (as we find in the Kings Survey-Booke of England) after the rate of fiftie and foure Hides: and had in it threescore and three Burgers. The Bishop of Winchester held it as Lord, and his courts or Pleas were kept here thrice in the yeere. And these Customes appertaine to Taunton, Burgerists, Theeves, Breach of peace, hansinare, pence of the Hundred, and pence of Saint Peter de Circieto, thrice in the yeere to hold the Bishops Plea without warning, to goe forth to warfare with the Bishops men. The Countrey here, most delectable on every side with green meadowes, flourishing with pleasant Gardens and Orchards, and replenished with fair Mannour houses; wonderfully contenteth the eyes of the beholders.*'

Canal, Bridgwater and Taunton

The Bridgwater and Taunton Canal enhanced an existing network of river navigation principally based on the River's Tone and Parrett.

Before the coming of the Bridgwater and Taunton Canal there was already in place an important navigation route from Bridgwater to Taunton along the river Tone and the River Parrett. Conservators administered Tone navigation, collecting tolls for maintenance and for the relief of the poor. Two acts were passed in 1699 and 1707 requiring the River Tone to be navigable from Taunton to Bridgwater. By 1823, 28,500 tons of coal was being carried to Taunton.

James Hollingsworth was the engineer for the canal which was built between 1823 and 1827, originally intended as part of an ambitious scheme to link the south coast of Devon and Bristol and avoid the lengthy and hazardous journey around Land's End. Originating at Taunton in Firepool and crossing Station Road by aqueduct, the canal joined the River Parrett at Huntworth. In 1832 Tone navigation was bought by the Bridgwater and Taunton Canal Company and in 1837 the canal was extended from Huntworth to Bridgwater. Robson's Directory of 1839 reports, 'The Bridgwater canal has given an impulse to its commerce by facilitating the transit of coals from Wales and the export of the agricultural produce of the adjacent country.' The four locks along the length of the canal beginning at the Taunton end are known as   Upper Maunsel, Lower Maunsel, Kings and Standards.

A dock was built in 1841 and an entrance lock to the River Parrett. A floating harbour meant that boats could be unloaded at any time of the day without regard to the tide. However, it did mean the increased use of the pumping station at Creech St Michael to prevent the silting-up of the dock. Before the opening of the dock the pumping station would mainly come into use in the summer when the Tone was generally at its lowest. It is thought that during periods of greatest demand, over 20 tons of coal was burnt a week in running the pumping station which could deliver 120,000 gallons of water an hour.

In 1866 the canal was sold to the Bristol and Exeter Railway Company for £64,000. It was the railway, of course, which meant the death of the canal as a commercial entity. However, on taking ownership the railway company built a new wharf at Bridgwater dock, perhaps seeing an integrated transport network as the future. After the Great Western Railway took over the Bristol and Exeter Railway Company in 1876, though, the canal went into a steep decline. This was further accelerated when the River Severn railway tunnel was opened in 1886. This meant that Welsh coal was no longer shipped over the Bristol Channel via Bridgwater Docks. The last barge tolls were collected in 1907.

In the second world war it served a new use as it became part of a defence line against German invasion along with the Chard Canal and the river Axe. The iron bridges were melted down and replaced with wooden ones which could be destroyed more quickly. Many of the pill boxes and tank traps which were built along the canal at this time survive (see Taunton Stop Line).

In 1947 the canal was taken over by the British Waterways board (later, British Waterways), and was used to provide extra water capacity for Durleigh Reservoir.

The Canal has now been fully restored along its 14.5 mile length by British Waterways in partnership with Somerset County Council and local district councils.

A narrow tub boat canal was built between 1831 and 1838 joining the River Tone at Taunton. There was also a cut to join the Tone at French Weir.

Carver, Richard (1796-1862)

Born in Bridgwater, he moved to Taunton in 1828 where he was county surveyor from 1830 until 1857. He was responsible for more than 20 new churches and alterations in Somerset including St Andrew's (Wiveliscombe, 1827-9), St Peter and St Paul's, (Bishop's Hull, 1825-7) and St George's (Wilton, 1837-9).

Castle

The origins of the castle lay in the building of a keep in 1138 by Henry of Blois, the Bishop of Winchester. It stood in the present day garden of the Castle Hotel. It was destroyed in 1155 by the new king, Henry II during Henry Blois's exile in France. At some point the keep was rebuilt.

The Great Hall was built in the 12th century and encompassed by a moat and administrative and domestic buildings. An outer moat ran along the line of what is now Corporation Street and the west side of part of North Street to Castle Bow, formerly the East Gate (which included a drawbridge and portcullis). Between the outer moat and the inner moat was a complex of buildings including stables, storehouses for grain, a dairy and a chapel (of St Peter). The West Gate of the castle, again with drawbridge, lay close to the current site of the Winchester Arms. There was a further drawbridge to enter the courtyard of the in-

ner ward. The castle owed much of its development to Bishop William Raleigh between 1246 and 1250. He provided a new hall, the Bishop's Chamber, a kitchen and associated buildings, and the chapel of St Nicholas.

The Castle was badly flooded in 1326. A regional parliament was held at the Castle in response to the threat of a French invasion on 10 March 1360. The Yorkist Thomas de Courtenay was holed up in the Castle by the Lancastrian, Lord Bonville in 1451.

A schoolhouse, the current municipal building in Corporation Street, was built at the instigation of Bishop Fox between 1521 and 1522.

Edward VI took over ownership of the Castle and Manor in 1551. In 1561, Queen Elizabeth leased the Castle and Manor to Sir Francis Knolleys. It briefly passed back to the crown before passing to Bishop Horne in 1575.

The Castle buildings had fallen into disrepair by the early 17th century when the Castle had become the responsibility of the bailiff and keeper of the castle. It was fortified with the onset of the Civil War in 1642. While under siege the Castle suffered severe damage, including to the Keep. However, it was quickly repaired. The Castle was taken from the Bishop of Winchester and granted to

Roger Hill of Poundsford in 1648. With the restoration in 1660 Charles ordered the destruction of Taunton Castle feeling no great love for Taunton and the part they had played in the parliamentarian cause, though it was only the ancient keep in the Castle Hotel grounds that was affected.

The Castle was eventually returned to the Bishop of Winchester and Walter Cliffe was granted the post of bailiff for the second time along with his son-in-law, John Beresford.

In 1685, following the Monmouth Rebellion in which Taunton played a pivotal role when the Duke of Monmouth, an illegitimate son of Charles II, sought to put himself on the throne instead of James II, the Great Hall of the Castle became the setting for the Bloody Assizes. It was presided over by the infamous Judge Jeffreys. He condemned 19 men to be hung in Taunton and a further 139 in the countryside round about.

By the time Sir Benjamin Hammett took on the responsibility for the Castle in 1786, the Castle was in a bad state of repair. Hammett repaired the Castle, made extensive alterations and filled in the moat.

The castle performed an important role in holding the Assizes and Quarterly Sessions, though this ceased in 1857 with the completion of the Shire Hall.

It then served as a venue for public events until, in danger of demolition, it was bought by the Somerset Archaeological and Natural History Society in 1874 to house its new museum. The Castle and the museum was leased to the County Council in 1958. A grade 1 listed building, it is (from 2008) undergoing an extensive program of restoration and improvement with money granted from the heritage lottery fund.

Castle Hotel

In about 1815 it was built as a private house for the Easton family, incorporating Castle Bow, the medieval east gate of the Castle. It was first an hotel in 1834 and by the 1st World War had become known as Clarke's Hotel. Charlotte Clarke had originally been the barmaid at the hotel but in 1850

The Castle Hotel

had been offered the hotel by the Lord of the Manor, Robert Mattock, and given time to find the money to pay him. This she was able to do by 1866 when she purchased the hotel outright. A third storey was added in the 1920's. It became the Castle Hotel in 1928.

In the early 1930's the garden was cleared to expose the Moat wall and the Keep originally dating back to the 12th century. Of particular interest is the square Norman Well. There are believed to be only two other examples in the country.

The Chapman family have run the hotel for over 50 years and it is currently owned by Christopher Chapman. It has become one of the top places to dine in the country, cultivating as it has, young talented chefs including Gary Rhodes, Phil Vickery and the current incumbent, Richard Guest. It holds the coveted Michelin Star and 3 AA rosettes.

A leaflet of 1786 advertising the services of the Castle Hotel

Census, 1841 & After

The census's of 1801, 1811 and 1831 were the responsibility of the overseers of the poor and the clergy and many of the returns were destroyed. The 1841 census was the first where the returns were the responsibility of the registrars who kept certificates for births, marriages and deaths. The questions were also more detailed and wide-ranging. The census for Taunton provides a fascinating insight into Taunton at this time.

Employment

The amount of people involved in services in 1841 was about 30% of the working population, higher than the rate employed in agriculture (25%) and manufacturing (25%), though we tend to think of the dominance of the service sector as a more recent phenomenon. This was due to the large number employed as domestic servants. Out of a population of 12,066 there were 946 domestic servants. Then came general labourers (439), silk manufacture employees (303), boot and shoe makers (291), agricultural labourers (164) and mason and stone-cutters (119).

The amount involved in manufacturing at 20% was below the national average of 31%. This did not significantly change until after 1925 and remained at around 20% throughout the 1950's and 1960's and 1970's before a steep decline from 1975, in general mimicking the decline nationally. In the 2001 census the amount employed in manufacturing was 11% compared with the national average of 16%.

The amount employed in agriculture at 25% was significantly more than the national average of 20%. Growth in the manufacturing economy, particularly in the midlands and the north, meant that the percentage employed in agriculture was already in decline. In Taunton, however, it was not until the latter part of the 19th century that there began a steady decline in agricultural employment, accelerating with the rapid increase in mechanisation in the 20th century. Now it stands below the national average of 2%.

Construction is an area that has varied little in the percentage of workers employed in it both locally and nationally. In 1841 it was just over 8% (2% higher than the national average) of which the number employed as Stonemasons was significant. It has never fallen below 6% in that time and is currently a little under 8%.

Unemployment
The first census for which we have accurate records of unemployment rates is the 1931 census which took place in the middle of the great depression when unemployment rates were historically high. The national rate at this time was 12.5%. In Taunton, though, it was 5.8% and throughout the years has always remained below the national average. In fact, Taunton's worst period of unemployment was during the eighties and early nineties when it reached nearly 10% in 1991. Since then it has steadily declined to around 2% in 2008.

Education
About 50% of children went to school at all in 1851 where as in 2008 about 76% of 16-17 year olds stay on at school. In 1951, only 2.5% stayed on in high school education beyond the age of 20 while in 2001, 19% have degrees or similar qualifications (slightly below the national average).

Life and Death
Infant mortality rates shown by the 1851 census were truly shocking. One in eight children would die in child-birth in Taunton. This was, however, better than the national average which was closer to one in six deaths during child-birth. Given that this was in part related to social class and poverty in some families the equation was far worse.

Religion.

There was no question about religion in the 1841 census though in 1851 at the time of the main census there was a seperate Census of Religion. In 1851 70% of the population of Taunton attended Church of England churches. The second highest were the Methodists, closely followed by the Baptists. Catholic attendance was 1.5%. There was an assumption that everyone was Christian in the 1851 census, so there was no provision for other religions or non-believers. The only other census in which a question on religion was asked was the 2001 census. In 2001, just over 15% said they had no religion (slightly above the national average). In 2001, 75% termed themselves as Christian, again slightly higher than the national average. The next largest representation was the Muslim religion at a little less than half-a-percent (2.78% nationally). Other religions represented were Jewish at 0.6% (2.78% nationally), Buddhist at 0.16% (0.27% nationally) and Hindu at 0.13% (1% nationally).

Housing

Though some statistics were asked on housing as early as 1891, they related mainly to the number of rooms and persons per household. From 1931 information on the total number of households was kept and, from 1951, the number of amenities. A key indicator was whether a house had a WC or not.

Year	Total Households	No WC
1931	15,250	-
1951	20,017	4,634
1971	27,414	2,579
1981	31,755	820
1991	38,104	405
2001	43,880	163

Charters

In 904 Edward the Elder met with Bishop Denewulf at Winchester in Bickleigh in Devon. The Bishop gave land in Somerset and other parts of the West Country in return for a right to the profits generated by Taunton and its territories. The people of Taunton were no longer required to pay certain taxes and perform certain duties for the King and his retinue and the Bishop of Winchester was given permission to raise market tolls and burgage rents. The ownership of Taunton and its territories by the Bishop of Winchester was cemented later in the century under King Edgar and

Bishop Aethwold along with particular judicial rights which meant the populace of Taunton were subject to the rule of the Bishops of Winchester in the way that others were subject to the King. By the mid tenth century Taunton had its own mint.

The first borough charter was granted by King Stephen in 1136. This gave exemptions from tolls, up to that time a concession only enjoyed by London and Winchester, and almost twenty years before Bristol was given such rights. The granting of the charter may well have resulted from the influence of Henry de Blois. It encouraged Taunton to trade more widely over a greater distance. The development of trade is indicated by two fairs that appear during that period. The first was held on 17 June and was dedicated to St Botolph. It is believed to have begun in the 13th century, though we have no precise date for its origin, and to have taken place in

We have inspected also the charter which our same progenitor (Stephen) granted to the bishop of the aforesaid place (Winchester) and to his men of Taunton in these words
Stehoen King of the English to his justices and sheriffs and barons and ministers and to his faithful people of all England and of the sea ports , Greeting
I command that all the burgesses of Taunton, the men of the Bishop of Winchester may have all the immunities and such privileges throughout my whole land of toll and passage dues and of every other custom, as to my burgesses of London and of Winchester have. And if anyone afterwards in defiance of this precept shall do them injury or insult, my justice and sheriffs may show that they have such immunities and customs. And in defiance of this no one shall disturb them or their affairs wrongfully under the penalty of ten pounds
Witness Robert de Ver
Milo de GLoucester

Left, photographic copy of the entry of the charter of Stephen to the men of Taunton recorded in the volume of Winchester Charters kept at the British Museum, and above, the translation. Probably written about the middle of the 13th century.

the Old Market Place, now the Parade. The second, dedicated to St Thomas Becket, was granted by Henry III in 1256 and took place on about the 7 July at Mill Lane.

In 1627 Taunton was given a new Royal Charter, giving the town an administrative body independent of the Bishop of Winchester with a Corporation and a Mayor. This had the effect of eroding the power and influence of the Bishop of Winchester. However, following the pivotal support of Taunton for the parliamentarians against the Royalists during the civil war (1642-6), the charter was taken away again in 1661.

After two more attempts at petitioning for a new charter in 1669 and 1675, a new charter was finally granted in 1677. The borough boundaries were enlarged and civil government was put into the hands of the Mayor, Town Clerk, Recorder, Aldermen and Burgesses of the Borough. It was, though, weighted in favour of the crown. The Recorder and the Town Clerk were hand-picked and only those taking the Oath of Allegiance were eligible to be elected to the council.

The charter was renewed by James II in 1688, increasing the King's influence once more. The charter lapsed in 1792, after a quarrel between Dr Cabbell (who was about to retire as Mayor) and Sir Thomas Gunston over the choice of a new Recorder. On the 28 August the Mayor and ten burgesses met and elected Sir Thomas as the new Mayor. However, when the new Mayor was about to be sworn in by Dr Cabbell on 1 November, he instead served him a notice saying that he could not swear him in 'because at the time your supposed election took place, there was not in existence a major part of the select body of the corporation.' Sir Thomas applied for a writ of *mandamus* to the King's Bench to compel Dr Cabbell to swear him into office. However, this was to no avail and, once again, Taunton was to lose its charter.

The final charter was granted in 1877. Until this time the town was effectively run by the Market Trustees, elected in 1768 to administer the area around the Parade, and the Board of Health (established in 1849). Under the new charter the corporation now consisted of a Mayor and six aldermen and the borough was divided into three wards.

Cinema

In the mid 1930's there were five full-time Cinemas in Taunton.

Exchange Theatre
(Picturedrome)

A cinema was established in the Corn Exchange building near Castle Bow in early 1910. It was originally known as the Picturedrome. In the morning

the building was used for commerce so each day the seating would have to be put out for the matinee. By the beginning of the war it was the Exchange Electric Theatre. The lease changed hands from a Mr A. Hope Parker to a Mrs Rouse who converted it to talkies in 1932. When the cinema converted to talkies admission prices rose from 3d to 6d. It closed in 1933.

Site of the Exchange Theatre cinema. The Corn Exchange building in which the cinema was located was pulled down and replaced by an Electricty Board Showroom and is now a Next outlet.

County Cinema

By the autumn of 1910 the Victoria Assembly Rooms in the London Hotel were also showing silent films on a daily basis. At this time it was known as the more racy Empire Electric Theatre. By the time it began showing talkies after a British Talking Pictures sound system was introduced in 1929 it had changed its name to the County Cinema (as it had to the County Hotel). The licensee was George Vickery. An unusual aspect of the cinema was that it used back projection. This was because it was part of the hotel and their was no room to build on a projection room.

The Lyceum

The Lyceum has a long and diverse history. It opened on Monday 18 August 1913 at the junction of Staplegrove Road and Station Road at the site of the Old George Inn at the behest of a consortium of local businessmen at a cost £3,500. The architects were Stone and Lloyd. It also doubled as a theatre with six dressing rooms. Sarah Bernhardt, Vesta Tilley and Hillaire Belloc all performed there. There were 500 seats at 3d and 6d. It was a shilling for the extra comfy seats at the rear. The seating capacity was later increased to

678 and a cafe was installed. After flirting with several different owners, it became the Odeon in 1937 and then the Classic in 1967. A second small screen with 71 seats was introduced in 1971. It was taken over by the Canon Group in 1988 but then closed in the autumn of 1990. Taunton was without any cinema for the first time since 1910! Then in 1992, as they had done originally, a consortium of local businessmen became involved and it re-opened as The Plaza. Les Laverock, the former manager, returned. However, its revival was short-lived. Within weeks of the opening of the new Odeon Multiplex at Hankridge Farm, it

closed, on 25 August 1994. The building was raised to the ground. A block of flats has been built in its place.

The Gaiety
The Gaiety opened in 1920 in Rowbarton near the station on the site of some former agricultural barns. One unique selling point was the serving of tea and biscuits and other beverages while seated. It was very early into talkies in October 1929 showing The Singing Fool with Al Johnson. A balcony was added in 1938 and the auditorium was lengthened so that the seating capacity increased to 672. A cafe was also installed. Further seats were added after the war to give a seating capacity of 791. In 1950 the owner Edward Vickery retired and the cinema was sold to the Cheltenham Cinema Company Ltd. It closed in 1963.

The Gaumont Palace
Situated in Corporation Street, it was opened on 11 July 1932 by the Mayor, W. E. Maynard and Jessie Matthews, the musical star who was at the height of her fame. It was a luxurious cinema with turquoise and gold dominating the colour scheme. It also housed a cafe. It had the largest screen in Somerset at the time as well as stage facilities to match. It also, unusually, had two seperate entrances. The proscenium was 54 feet wide and there were eight dressing rooms. It could seat 1,476. It shortened its name to the Gaumont in 1940 when ownership passed to Albany Ward Cinemas. In the 1950's Cinemascope was introduced and the seating capacity was increased to 1500. In 1962, now part of the J. Arthur Rank Organisation, it became the New Odeon. Over the years it hosted many big names on its stage including The Beatles and The Rolling Stones. It closed to Herbie Goes Bananas in 1981 and became a Bingo Hall.

The Odeon (Hankridge Farm)

The Odeon multiplex cinema opened at Hankridge Farm in August 1994 with five screens. At the time it was only the ninth multiplex that the Rank Organisation had installed. Three more screens were subsequently added. Seating capacity ranges from 88 to 334 seats.

A more traditional cinema experience can still be found at the Wellesley Cinema in nearby Wellington, built in 1937 in the Art Deco style.

Coat of Arms

The coat of arms for Taunton is not the original one. It was altered in 1934.

Original Coat of Arms dating from 1685 or before   *Current Coat of Arms date from 1934*

The Taunton coat of arms are on a background of blue with a gold cherub at the top and a Saxon crown at the bottom. It is surmounted by a peacock (on top of the crown). The arms date from October 1934 when they were granted by the College of Arms. They replaced an earlier design which depicted the imperial crown. This could only be borne by the special permission of the monarch and was changed to a Saxon one. The first known reference to a coat of arms is in 1685. It is thought that they were adopted after the towns charter was restored in 1677. The motto is Defendamus (We shall defend). It is often considered a reference to Taunton's refusal to surrender to Royalist forces during the civil war, however, it appears on the seal of Taunton, the original of which is dated 1685, a time when the corporation was pro-Royalist (even if a large number of the population of the town was not). It may just as well, therefore, be a statement that it is the duty of the town to stand by its King.

The Borough Seal

Coins & tokens

Normanby Hoard

A hoard of Roman coins was discovered in Holway in 1821. In total 430 coins were listed as being found but it is suspected that there were far more. A number of coins from private collections have found their way into the museums over the years. The coins are of the late 4th century.

Civil War Coin Hoard

In 1980 a hoard of silver coins was discovered by Graham Sully while driving a JCB during construction work at Hawkes's Yard, 32 East Street. The find was unusual in the number of high value coins found. They were stored in a pot away from the house (unfortunately the pot did not survive). It is believed that they were hidden around the time of the Civil War (1642-51) in which Taunton took such an active part. This may well account for the hiding place and the

Mark Antony, 44 - 31 BC

high value of the coins. Of the 275 silver coins found, 268 were shillings, six were half-crowns and one was a crown. They date back to Edward VI. Other monarchs represented on the coins are Philip & Mary, Elizabeth I, James I

Coin of Elagubalus, AD 218-222. Depicts Mars, god of war carrying a spear and trophy.

and Charles I. They were mainly minted at the tower Mint in London. The crown, however, was minted at the Truro mint, which is unusual. The coins were purchased by the Somerset County Museum for £3,335.

The Shapwick Coin Hoard

In September 1998 the largest hoard of Roman silver denarii ever discovered in Britain was found at Shapwick (between Bridgwater and Street) by two cousins, Martin and Kevin Elliott, who made the find whilst metal detecting. 9,238 coins were discovered. This is three times bigger than the pervious record hoard at Colchester.

The coins were buried in the room of a previously undiscovered Roman building which proved to be part of a courtyard villa. The coins are thought to have been buried in about AD 24. Though the majority of coins were minted in Rome others may have been struck in Greece, Syria and Alexandria.

The coins included, among others, the reigns of Mark Antony, Nero, Vespasian, Titus, Marcus Aurelius, Commodus, Septimius Severus, Caracalla, Elagabalus and Severus Alexander.

The value of the hoard, which represents more the ten years pay for a legionary at that time, suggests that the coins were intended to be used to pay the army or the local civil service.

West Bagborough Hoard.
A hoard of 4th century Roman silver was discovered by James Hawkesworth in October 2001, whilst metal detecting in a field near Bagborough. A total of 681 silver coins were discovered. They chiefly covered the reigns of Emperor Constantius II (337 - 361) and Emperor Julian (331/2 - 363 AD). The coins were struck in France (Arles and Lyons) and Germany (Trier) as well as Rome.

Taunton Tokens of the 17th century
A number of tradesmen's tokens were issued in the 17th century. The coins, which were made from copper, took the name of the tradesman or, sometimes, the constable of the town. Fifty issuers were identified in Taunton. The majority have been tracked down through the Hearth Tax Return of 1664-5 which, unusually, listed taxpayers by the Street they lived in.

19th Century Tokens (or checks)
The majority of tokens (known as checks), though not all, were issued in the second half of the 19th century. The co-operative society were the most active in issuing types of token. They were used as a means of recording how much a customer had spent and would be exchanged when a dividend was due. They were also used for the pre-payment of goods to the door. Other retailers also used them, such as tea dealers, chemists, jewellers and fish mongers, often as a type of loyalty or bonus scheme.

Public house tokens were prevalent in the last quarter of the 19th century when alcohol consumption was at a historic high. Very often their use seems to have been associated with games, such as skittle and quoits, both very popular at this time. Typically the tokens would be purchased in advance and given as a reward to the victors to be exchanged for beer. There are also examples of their use as a reward to volunteers for fighting a fire or for soldiers on the move. Most of the tokens, which in most cases were metal (mainly brass and copper), were not dated.

Tokens from Clarke's Hotel

Examples of the above coins and tokens are normally on view at the County Museum in Taunton Castle.

Collins, Victor (1903-1971)
Taunton's first and (so far) only Labour MP.

He defeated the Conservative Colonel Wickham in the landslide general election of 5 July 1945. He described it as one of the proudest and happiest moments of his life. The 1950 general election brought Winston Churchill to the town and he lost his seat to the Conservative Henry Hopkinson (later Lord Colyton) in a close fought contest by 20,724 votes to 19,352. He did, however, win the seat for Shoreditch and Finsbury in a by-election in 1954 after the death of the incumbent Labour MP Ernest Thurtle. He was elevated to the House of Lords in July 1958 as one of the first fourteen life peers. He opposed Beeching's proposed railway cuts in 1963 and served under the Wilson government between 1964 and 1970, first as a junior minister in the Home Office and later as Minister of State before becoming a Privy Councillor in 1969.

Colthurst, Francis (1879-1945)

He was born in 1874, the oldest of nine children of George Edward Colthurst who owned the timber yard in Taunton in Staplegrove Road. The timber yard closed after the building of a supermarket store in the 1990's. His father, rather unselfishly, encouraged him to train as an artist rather than go into the family firm. He studied at Taunton and then at the National Art Training School where he was awarded silver and bronze medals. He taught art at Regent Street Polytechnic and was exhibited at the royal Academy twelve times. He travelled and painted in Spain, Italy, Morocco and Holland. He eventually became a member of the Royal Academy. He also collected Chinese ceramics. Part of his collection was left to the Somerset Archaeological and Natural History Society and has been on display at Taunton Castle Museum.

Sketch of waiter in Toledo by Francis Colthurst

Convent

The Convent building was originally built as a hospital in 1772 before passing into private hands. It was bought by nuns of the Order of St Francis in 1807, emigres from Brussels during the French Revolution..

They spent £5,656 17s 2d on converting the building and adding a new wing before completing the move from Winchester.

In 1809 an organ was installed in the school room which served as a temporary chapel. In 1810 an adjoining field was purchased and in 1811 a chapel was built.

A Catholic boarding school was opened and named St Francis School. The fees in the early years were £40 a year. There were no holidays and the days were long with little recreation time, mimicking the nuns long working day.

In 1812 a free day school was opened for the Catholic school girls. When the Catholic Chapel opened in the Crescent in 1822 the pupils from the day school were taken there on Sunday. The nuns could not attend because they had vows of enclosure.

In 1845 a walled field was bought adjacent to the convent grounds to give the convent a total area of about 14 acres. Cattle and pigs, and later, hens and ducks were kept and a dairy farm was established. A new wing was built in 1853 as the number of novices and nuns increased. Cloisters were also added to enclose the burial ground in 1860.

As a free school was no longer required with the advent of universal free education, consideration was given to a fee paying school for the middle classes. A new school wing was built in 1865 and opened as St Joseph's Middle School, to provide

The Horarium (or daily schedule)

In her History of the Convent in Taunton, Rosemary Berry describes the nun's working day.

'They would start the day very early, rising at 5 a.m'. After washing in cold water they would dress and engage in private prayer, reading or work before proceeding to the chapel for Prime where 'The coming of light into the world was the chief symbolism, and the new day was dedicated to God.' After mass at 7.15 came a breakfast 'of bread and butter (or later margerine) and home-brewed beer (later replaced by tea and coffee)'. Work at various tasks followed at 9 o'clock followed by half-an-hour of mental prayer. They worked from 9.00 to 11.30. when they would break for dinner. 'Dinner consisted of vegetables grown in the kitchen gardens, meat on Tuesdays and Sundays, or eggs and cheese from the dairy.' From mid-day to 3.45 they would work before returning to the chapel for Vespers and Compline. This was followed by mental prayer and benediction and then collation (supper) at 5 p.m. From 6-7 p.m. they could relax in the workroom, 'Here the nuns would read, write, draw, paint, write letters and converse.' Then came 'The Great Silence', Rosary and Matins and Lauds 'in anticipation of dawn of the next day'.At 10 p.m. all retired to bed.

The work referred to could involve a number of tasks principally revolving around the kitchen, the gardens and domestic houshold chores, or teaching.

education for Catholic girls. Another 10 acres was acquired for the farm in 1864 and a farmhouse was built in 1868. More fields were bought and by 1883 the convent and grounds extended to the Mount. Part of this land was given over to the building of St George's Church in 1858 and St George's School in 1870.

Mother Francis Agnes Jerningham had been head of the convent for 46 years when she died on 15 April 1883. She was succeeded by Mother Gertrude Therry.

From 1900 to 1911 a residential course was held on practical housekeeping for 'Ladies of the Upper Classes.' This was held at a newly completed house adjacent to the convent called St Anne's. In 1948 St Francis's School became a Preparatory School for girls aged 7-13..

By 1953 the numbers in the convent had declined so much that the Franciscan community left the Convent. The majority moved to Arundel in West Sussex. They took the Rule of St. Clare and became Poor Clares.

THE KIDNAPPER.—A CASE FOR THE POLICE.

Above, cartoon from Punch. The caption read, 'There's a beautiful veil!!!Give me your parcel my dear while you put it on.

One of the greatest tests for the convent was over the welfare of Augusta Talbot. She was the daugher of the Hon. George Talbot, niece of the Earl of Shrewsbury and was a pupil at St Francis School. Both her parents had died when she was young and she was in the care of Father Thomas Doyle who had arranged her schooling at the Convent. When her brother also died she was heir to £85,000, a fortune then, which was held in trust until she was 21 and married. Her stepfather, the Hon. Fitzharding Berkeley, tried to aquire her fortune and began a chancery suit against Father Doyle in 1851. Her aunt, Lady Shrewsbury tried to persuade her to marry a cousin, an Italian Count, to keep the fortune in the family. When Augusta refused she left for Italy in a huff and Augusta was received into the convent in South Road as a temporary postulant for her protection. The motives of the convent were questioned, particularly in the Times and a cruel cartoon in Punch Magazine. There was still a deal of strong anti-Catholic feeling in the country at this time. However, the law suit by Fitzharding Berkeley was rejected, following a visit to the convent. When Augsusta married Lord Howard she gave two statues to the convent in gratitude for her protection.

However, this was not the end of the convent story. It was taken on by the Sisters of St Joseph of Annecy, an order founded in France in 1650. Some of the Sisters were already established in Taunton and some of them had already spent some time as guests at the Convent and in residence at number 8 Mountfields.

The Convent School continued, now renamed St. Joseph's Convent School. The school was updated and modernised and both the convent school and the Preparatory School proved very popular. It thrived in the 1960's but numbers declined in the 1970's. It stopped taking borders and closed in 1978.

The School was acquired by King's College and Tuckwell House and Neate's House were established as part of the King's College School.

In 2004 the site began its latest incarnation as it began to be converted into residential flats.

County Hotel

Formerly known as The Three Cups, The London Inn and the London Hotel, the County Hotel was centre stage to many of the events in Taunton's history until its sale and the opening of retail units in 1995.

The first known reference is from a licence to bake bread at the Three Cups in 1528.

During the Civil War the inn was owned by a wealthy Exeter merchant called John Mallack. The hotel was partly destroyed in the defence of Taunton. Mallack, a Royalist Captain was fined a tenth of the value of the property following the Parliamentarian victory. He was succeeded by his son, also Roger, who, in turn was succeeded by his son, Rawlin who became MP for Ashburton.

During the Monmouth Rebellion, the Duke of Monmouth lodged at John Hucker's house opposite the Three Cups. In the early 18th century the Inland Revenue based themselves within the Inn and, in September 1743, John Wesley stayed there on one of his visits to Taunton.

In March 1773 a new landlord, Samuel Granger, arranged for a visiting drama company to put on a play (The Clandestine Marriage), a concert and an opera. He rebuilt the inn to the design that endured until the closure of the hotel. It was re-opened in March 1784.

It was renamed 'The London Inn' by Thomas Baldon, who took it over in 1784. Under the ownership of a consortium of three doctors (William Kinglake, James Cole and James Bryant) it became the headquarters of the local military.

After being bought by William Sweet in 1799 it closed as an inn for 15 years until, in 1814, William Willie, set about restoring its fortune. He persuaded the High Sheriff, John Phelps, to make the inn his residence during the Taunton Assizes of March 1815, started a new coach service to London that only took 26 hours, held balls in the long room and hosted large dinners for members of parliament. He raised a mortgage to buy the freehold from his landlord. However, his superficial success hid a financial mess. The inn changed hands again. The tenant from 1829, Samuel Jeffrey, changed the name to the London Hotel.

Jeffrey was succeeded by James Govier between 1834 and 1838, during which time the Liberal Henry Labouchere held a victory dinner after the defeat of the young Benjamin Disraeli. In 1841 following the purchase of the hotel by Charles Hutchins of Sherborne and the installation of a new tenant, George Coombe, the hotel became the home of the Conservative Association. When Coombe died in May 1846 his sister inherited and married the wealthy Thomas Meetens who built a new assembly room where he held a number of successful events. Such was the success that the Assembly Rooms were extended further. Plays, concerts, operas and lunches to mark major events all took place there.

When Meetens retired in 1869 the new purchaser, Samuel Tyzack, continued in the same spirit. In particular he invited some of the famous singers of the day and local groups such as the Taunton Musical Society and the Taunton Philharmonic Association to put on events. In 1876 Daniel Nash took over the hotel for two years to be followed by Henry Steed. There were some notable events held here during his time including talks by the African explorer and journalist H. M. Stanley and Dr Barnardo, and a performance of H.M.S. Pinafore by the D'Oyly Carte Opera.

The County Hotel, now retail units, at the heart of events in Taunton for over 400 years

When Steed sold to Henry Gill in September 1887 for £6,000, he put his nephew, George Saunders in place as the proprietor. Its role as a centre for entertainment and high profile events continued. A notable feature was the production of an opera based on the events of the siege of Taunton in the Civil War 'In the Days of the Siege - A Romance of Taunton'. When it was revived in 1900 to raise money for reservists fighting in the Boer War it marked the first production of the Taunton Operatic Society. It was during the Boer War, in January 1901, that the hotel was bought by Ernest Claridge of Bristol. He added a permanent stage, dressing rooms and an enlarged auditorium. Fred Karno, Edgar Wallace, the Souza Band and George Grossmith all performed there. The hotel was also host to several moving panorama shows as well as numerous exhibitions, fund-raising events and political gatherings from both the main parties. In 1910 it showed its first moving picture which eventually eclipsed the moving panoramas.

The hotel was taken over by Frederick Whittingham when Claridge sold the hotel to become a farmer. It then became the property of Trust Houses Ltd. This was when it changed its name to the County Hotel. Balls and events continued to be held in the Assembly Rooms. When the cinema began showing talkies the cinema changed its name from the Empire Electric to the County Cinema, though it was to close soon afterwards in October 1934.

With the advent of the Second World War, the hotel once again hosted several events in connection with raising money and morale for the war effort, as well as a number of concerts. In 1950, following the defeat of the Tory candidate in the 1945 election to the Labour Candidate Victor Collins, Churchill came to Taunton and addressed 1,000 people in the Empire Hall (formerly the Assembly Rooms). It continued to host a number politicians from the three main parties following refurbishment in 1960, as well as a number of other events.

Cox, Serjeant E. W.

The first editor of the *Somerset County Gazette* between 1836 and 1845. He was also a lawyer in Hammet Street and owner of the The Times and The Field and founder of the Exchange & Mart Magazine. He bought the Lordship of the Manor of Taunton from the executors of the will of Robert Mattock. On his death it passed to his son Irwin Cox MP.

Cranmer, Thomas (1489-1556)

Thomas Cranmer was appointed as Archdeacon of Taunton it would seem as a reward for the role he played in attempting to secure the divorce of Henry VIII from Catherine of Aragon.

He advised Henry that he should appeal to the Universities of Christendom and helped compile the Collectanea Satis Copiosa (the sufficiently abundant collection) in which it was suggested that there was a precedent for such a case as Henry's. He went to Rome to gain sympathy for the case in 1530 and later that year was appointed as Archdeacon of Taunton.

When Archbishop William Wareham, the Archbishop of Canterbury, died in 1532, Cranmer was appointed in his place, a position he would hold for the next 23 years. In this position he annulled the marriage of Catherine of Aragon which led the way for Henry to marry Anne Boleyn. This led to his excommunication as well as that of Henry.

This, of course, was just the beginning of Cranmer's involvement. He later annulled Henry's marriage to Anne Boleyn and divorced him from Anne of Cleves. When Edward Seymour took over the running of the country on Henry VIII's death in 1547 on behalf of the young Edward, he supported a move to Protestantism and the translation of the Bible into English. He was responsible for converting the mass into communion, two new prayer books (in 1459 and 1552) and the 42 articles of religion (in 1553). On Edward Seymour's death he supported the succession of his daughter-in-law, Lady Jane Grey. This only lasted nine days. She was forced to abdicate in favour of Mary Tudor, Edward's half-sister. She sent Cranmer to the tower and he was burnt at the stake on 21 March 1556.

Cromwell, Thomas (c1485-1540)

As Thomas Cranmer was appointed Archdeacon of Taunton as a reward, a seat as an MP was made for Cromwell in Taunton in 1529, a year after the death of his wife. This was the year that the influential Cardinal Wolsey fell from grace over his inability to persuade the pope to grant a divorce from Catherine of Aragon. The seat found for Cromwell as an MP for Taunton enabled him to remain in government service. By 1532 he had become the King's chief minister and was a leading figure among those who suggested Henry make himself head of the English church. He presided over the dissolution of the monasteries with great efficiency and was created Earl of Essex in 1540. However, also like Cranmer, he came to a sticky end. It was his support for the marriage of Henry to Anne of Cleves in the hope of cementing an alliance of North German Princes against the Holy Roman Emperor that led to his downfall. Both the marriage and the alliance failed. Cromwell was charged with treason and executed at the Tower of London on 28 July 1540.

Crosse, Andrew (1784-1855)

In the forefront of experiments with electricity, he was embroiled in controversy at local level and then at national level for 'playing god' and may also have been the inspiration for Mary Shelley's Frankenstein.

In 1839 Andrew Crosse of nearby Fyne Court performed an experiment in Taunton. The Times described how 'He illuminated 400 feet of iron chain, hung in festoons about the room, the whole extent being brilliantly lighted at the same instant by the passage through it from the spark from the battery, and melted several feet of wire. Mr Crosse afterwards detailed the results of many experiments on thunder clouds and mists by means of a wire apparatus suspended in his park and there was an incessant stream from his conductor of sparks, each one of which would have struck an elephant dead in an instant.'

An experiment which he conducted three years earlier embroiled him in a controversy which has not been fully resolved to this day.

He had been passing an electrical current through a porous volcanic rock saturated in a strong solution in an attempt to produce crystals. Crystals did not form but he noticed white 'excrescences' forming on the stone. On the 26th day of the experiment he saw what he described as 'the perfect insect'. His initial thought was that his experiment had been contaminated by insect eggs. However, when he repeated the experiment a number of times in a controlled environment he produced the same results. He did not tell anybody until he met his friend the poet Robert Southey walking on the Quantock Hills. On his advice he carefully documented the experiment and sent the results to the London Electrical Society. They asked the renowned W. H. Weekes to repeat the experiment using Crosse's notes. No doubt to their surprise, the results were the same. The implications were enormous: that he was able to create life. A local reporter for the Somerset County Gazette got hold of the story. It was then taken up by the Times and other national newspapers. He was accused of 'playing god'

> To some of the local farmers he was the thunder and lightning man

and by some of being an atheist. He received many angry letters. Crosse was not interested in personal fame and was stung by the criticism. He became, for the most part, a recluse, though he was defended by no lesser a figure than the scientist Michael Faraday.

Crosse's fascination with electricity began early and in some ways is not surprising, born as he was to a father who was a notable scholar whose acquaintances included Benjamin Franklin and Joseph Priestly, early pioneers in the field of electricity. When he was sent to school at the Fort in Bristol he obtained permission to go to some lectures on natural science including a lecture on electricity.

After his father died when he was only 16 he went to Oxford to study the classics though he would have preferred to have studied science. Soon after completing university at 21 a further tragedy occurred when his mother died. He was now in charge of the estate.

He met up with a fellow electrical enthusiast, George Singer while in London. They became close friends. One of his particular interests was the study of electricity in the atmosphere and to this end he ran copper wire extending to a third of a mile around trees and poles. It connected to a capacitor next to his laboratory which would be charged when the atmospheric conditions were favourable. To some of the local farmers he was the 'thunder and lightning man' who was responsible for poor crops and at night at his home 'devils, all surrounded by lightning, dancing on the wire'. However, he had a positive local image too. His electrical apparatus had sometimes been used for medical purposes when locals would come to be cured of their aches and pains. There was one particular account of a man who had apparently been cured of paralysis down his left side after a session of six weeks of such treatment.

He was visited by Humphry Davy who was president of the Royal Society and noted in the field of electro-chemistry. In 1836 he spoke at a meeting of the British Association for the Advancement of Science at Bristol on electricity and crystal formation. Sir Richard Phillips visited and was amazed at the variety of apparatus. He sometimes improvised and when he was short of porcelain or

glass containers for making batteries, he would lop the head off an empty wine bottle and use that instead.

He may also have been the inspiration for Mary Shelley's novel *Frankenstein*. She is thought to have attended at least one of his lectures at Garnerin's, a popular lecture room in London in 1814. Her novel was published in 1818.

His wife and his brother died in 1846 but he was to marry again in 1850 to Cornelia Bradley, a young

Fyne Court, now part of the National Trust.

woman he had met in London. It is to her after his death in July 1855 aged 71 that we owe our knowledge of much of his work. She put together two books on his experiments from notes and scraps of paper. Throughout his life he was reluctant to write up his own work or have it published.

His interests were not just confined to science He loved the natural landscape of the Quantocks, had a great interest in the welfare of the poor, opened small copper mines in Broomfield and used his electrical knowledge to conduct electro-therapy treatments on those suffering from rheumatism, arthritis or paralysis (as indicated above). He also wrote a great deal of poetry.

The house at Fyne Court, unfortunately, was almost entirely destroyed by fire in 1894. However, the remaining buildings and grounds are now owned by the National Trust and part of his laboratory has been re-created there.

Cudgel Playing & Devonshire Wrestling

Goldsworthy in his Recollections of Old Taunton gives a vivid account of the deceptively playful sounding cudgel playing (or Single Stick as it was sometimes called) as practised in the early part of the 19 th century.

'Half-a-dozen casks were rolled on the Parade or some open place, on which were laid several wooden planks to form a platform, around which would gather the spectators. A man would then get upon it, take off his coat and hat, and flourish a stick around his head. Another fellow would throw his hat on the platform and do the same....Sticks would rattle, and blows would be parried, amidst noise, laughter, cursing, and swearing, until one of them had his "head broken", that is, until his scalp was laid open, 'Many must have been seriously hurt, and suffered more or less afterwards: the blows onto their heads and shoulders sounded very like striking with a stick a bole dish turned upside down. These amusements seldom ended without fights between the relations and friends of the players.'

Wrestlers came from Devonshire to challenge the local men, notable local wrestlers like Rab Channing and Tom Gainer.

Though Goldsworthy approved of wrestling in general 'as a healthy and useful exercise' he did not approve of the tendency to kick at each others shins 'with hobnailed and toe-tipt boots' He goes on, 'I have seen men kicking away at each others shins until they were scarcely able to stand from pain and loss of blood; when they could not get at each others shins, each would try to lift his opponent bodily off his legs and dash him with great force to the ground.'

Thomas Dare

Thomas Dare was a Taunton goldsmith who was, like many Taunton people of his day, against the future succession of James II.

He acquired fame in 1680 when he personally pressed a petition from the inhabitants of Taunton to this effect into the King's own hand outside the House of Lords.

When asked how he dare do such a thing he replied that his name was Dare. His cheek cost him a £500 fine. He fled to Amsterdam and accompanied the Duke of Monmouth when he landed at Lyme Regis in June 1685, only to be shot dead in a dispute over a horse.

Daniel Defoe (1659/1661-1731)

The author of Robinson Crusoe and Moll Flanders, he published his three volume Tour Round the Whole Island of Britain in 1727, a few years before his death.

The book is written in a series of letters. The following extract is from Volume 2, Letter 4, Part 2: Somerset and Wiltshire:

'I entered the county, as I observed above, by Wellington, where we had the entertainment of beggars; from whence we came to Taunton, vulgarly called Taunton Dean upon the River ton; this is a large, wealthy and exceedingly populous, town: one of the chief manufacturers of the town told us, that there was at that time so good a trade in the town, that they had then eleven hundred looms going for the weaving of sagathies, du roys, and such kind of stuffs, which are made there; and that which added to the thing very much, was, that not one of those looms wanted work: He farther added, that there was not a child in the town, or in the villages around it, of above five years old, but if it was not neglected by its parents, and untaught, could earn its own bread. This was what I never met with in any place in England, except at Colchester in Essex.

This town chooses two Members of Parliament, and their way of choosing is, by those who they call "pot-wallopers", that is to say, every inhabitant, whether house-keeper or lodger, that dresses their own victuals; to make out which, several inmates, or lodgers, will, sometime before the election, bring out their pots and make fires in the street, and boil their victuals in the sight of their neighbours, that their votes may not be called into question.

There are two large parish churches in the town, and two or three meeting-houses, whereof, one is said to be the largest in the county. The inhabitants have been noted for the number of Dissenters; for among them it was always counted a seminary of such: they suffered deeply in the Duke of Monmouth's Rebellion, but paid King James home for the cruelty exercised by Jeffreys among them; for when the Prince of Orange arrived, the whole town ran in to him, with so universal a joy, that, 'twas thought, if he had wanted it, he might have raised a little army there, and in the adjacent part of the country.

There was, and, I suppose, is still, a private college, or academy, for the Dissenters in this town; the tutor, who then managed it, was named Warren, who told me, that there were threescore and twelve ministers then preaching, whereof six had conformed to the Church, the rest were among the Dissenters, who had been his scholars, whereupon, one of his own sort had, it seems, styled him the Father of the Faithful: The academy, since his death, is continued, but not kept up to the degree it was, in the days of the said Mr Warren.'

Defendamus

Between 26 and 30 June 1928 there was a Grand Historical Pageant in Taunton entitled Defendamus.

*Major M. F. Cely Trevilian,
Master of the Pageant*

The Reverend D. P. Alford had written a sketch for a Taunton Pageant in 1910. This early sketch was built on and developed by Major M. F. Cely Trevilian and Laurance E. Tanner of Bristol who wrote the book and the music for the pageant.

In his introduction to the book printed to commemorate the event, Trevilian explains that the pageant 'must not be simply regarded as a play, the pageant of today traces its ancestry through the Elizabethan mask, the Tudor interlude, and the Medieval morality play back to the rites of Dionysus in Ancient Greece; and whatever name it took, its principle was always the same, namely to use the hand maid of religion or morality by means of using scenes of a historical or mythical character to illustrate some ethical teaching.' Moreover, 'The lesson which this pageant strives to teach is that of continuity. Our forefathers struggled each in their day to defend the right as it was given them to see it. It is for us to pass that heritage on to our children not only undiminished but enhanced.'

For Michael Woods, who wrote a study of the Pageant in 1999, it had a more divisive roll:

'By incorporating elements of ritual, spectacle and carnival, the Taunton Pageant promoted discourses of continuity and community which sought to reinforce the position of the local elite at a time of political instability and to reinforce conservative hegemony in mid-twentieth century rural Britain.' (Journal of Historical Geography, Academic Press, 1999).

Whichever it was, it was a large undertaking with a general purposes committee, an executive committee and six sub-committees. A book was produced of the pageant and some film still exists of the event.

The scenes were as follows:

TAUNTON
PAGEANT
JUNE 26 - 30 1928

Taunton: An A - Z

Prologue. Midsummer Night.
Part 1. Defence of Country.
       Episode 1. King Ina. 710.
       Episode 2. King Alfred & the Danes. 873.
       Scene 1. Athelney.
       Scene 2. Aller.
Part 2. Defence of Custom.
       Episode 3 The Manor of Taunton Deane. 1384.
       Episode 4. Perkin Warbeck. 1497.
Part 3. Defence of Law.
       Episode 5. The Siege of Taunton. 1645.
Part 5. Defence of Freedom.
       Episode 6. The Western Rebellion.
       Scene 1. The Blow. 1685. June.
       Scene 2. The Recoil. 1685. September.
Epilogue. Midsummer Night.

Taunton Anthem. Tanner and Trevilian respectively composed and wrote the words to a Taunton anthem to accompany the pageant. The rousing second verse is still sometimes sung on official occasions.

> *Monarch of our Vales and hillside,*
> *Spirit of love and land,*
> *Storied hero of old battles,*
> *Knightly heart and steadfast hand;*
> *Peerless Prince, hear now our promise*
> *On this night of hopes and fears*
> *For ourselves and our children*
> *Down the throbbing tale of years!*
>
> *Love of country, self forgetting;*
> *Equal Law for small or great;*
> *Custom, harbinger of freedom;*
> *Throned in worship, thought and state;*
> *These the lessons we must master,*
> *These the things which to the end -*
> *Though the heavens crash around us*
> *To the death we must defend!*
>
> *While the soft green hills caress us,*
> *While our dreaming river runs*
> *"Defendamus" - this the watchword*
> *For ourselves and our sons!*
> *And when we have learnt our lesson*
> *We shall look-and not in vain*
> *For they waking, royal Arthur!*
> *We shall serve with thee again!*

DE STAUNTON FOR TAUNTON!

De Staunton, William
William de Staunton was chosen as the first Taunton Member of Parliament, along with Humphrey Kael, in 1290.

Disraeli, Benjamin (1804 - 1881)
In later years Disraeli was to have a glittering political career, first as Chancellor and then as Prime Minister. However, in his early years he was struggling to establish his political credentials as an MP.

In 1835 Disraeli contested an election at Taunton as a Conservative having made two unsuccessful attempts as an Independent Radical at Wycombe in 1832 and 1835 and Marylebone in 1833. During the Taunton by-election Disraeli became involved in a ferocious quarrel with O'Connell over the latter's new alliance with the Whigs and Disraeli's move to the Conservatives. O'Connell spoke of 'the impenitent thief who died on the cross, and whose name, I verily believe, must have been Disraeli.' Disraeli challenged the son of O'Connell to a duel on behalf of his father. However, they both ended up being bound over to the peace. In the election he lost the Taunton seat to the incumbent Henry Labouchere (later Lord Taunton) by 452 votes to 282.

Domesday, in Taunton
The Domesday Book was a record of the country in the year 1086 prepared on the instruction of William the Conqueror. He wanted to know how much tax was due to him. The great manor of Taunton was the largest single estate in Somerset.

The following is an extract from a translation of the Domesday Book:

Taunton: An A - Z

'The Bishop of Winchester holds Taunton. Archbishop Strigand held it in the time of King Edward, and it paid the geld for fifty-four hides, and two yard-lands and a half, of which there was arable land sufficient for one hundred ploughs. Besides this the Bishop has in demsne twenty carucates which never paid the geld, and thirteen ploughs. There are eighty villains, eighty-two bordars, seventy bondmen or slaves, sixteen coliberti, and seven pound ten shillings, and amongst them all they have sixty ploughs.

There are sixty-four burgesses in Taunton who pay thirty-two shillings or six-pence each, to the Bishop of Winchester for his protection.

There are three mills which render ninety-five shillings.

The market yields fifty shillings.

There is a mint at Taunton which yields a profit of fifty shillings.

There are forty acres of meadow, a common of pasture two miles long and one mile broad; and a wood one mile in length and the same in breadth.

Fascimile of Somerset Domesday

When Bishop Walchelin received this manor it paid fifty pounds, it now pays one hundred and forty pounds and thirteen pence, with all its appendages and customs.

These are the customs of Taunton; Burgeristh, Latrones, Hundred-pence, Brach of the peace, Heinfare, Church-set, and St. Peters Pence, the tenants attend the Bishop's courts three times in the year being summoned, and go to the army with the Bishop's men.

The lands in the manor of Taunton subject to these customs are Tolland, Oake, Holford, Upper-Cheddon, Lower Cheddon, Maidenbrook, Langford, Bishop's Hull, and Heale, Ninehead, Norton Bradford, Halse, Heathfield, Shapnoller and Stoke; but the tenants of the two last are not liable to go to the army.

The tenants of Bagborough are subject to the same customs, except attendance on the army and on funerals.

The tenants of all these lands come to Taunton to swear fealty and to have justice administered; and when the lords of these lands die they are buried in Taunton. Bishop's Hull and Heale could not be seperated from Taunton in the time of King Edward.

Of the above said fifty hides and a half a yard of land, Geoffrey now holds four hides and a half; There are in demesne ten ploughs and twelve bondmen, twenty villains and twenty eight bordars or cottagers, with ten ploughs. There are thirty seven acres of meadow, and forty three acres of woodland, and a mill which belongs to the said Hugh, of the value of three shillings. The value of these lands altogether is twenty seven pounds.'

Du Cann, Edward Dillon Lott

Edward Du Cann was Taunton's youngest and longest serving MP.

He was elected as conservative MP for Taunton in a 1956 by-election following unsuccessful contests at Walthamstow West in 1951 and Barrow-in-Furness in 1955. He was MP for 31 years until his retirement in 1987.

He was Economic Secretary to the Treasury in 1962 and Minister of State at the Board of Trade from 1963-4. He was Chairman of the Conservative Party from 1965-7 and Chairman of the 1922 Committee from 1972 until 1984. He was Chairman of the Public Accounts Committee between 1974-9.

He came out against membership of the of the EEC during the 1975 referendum.

He was also company director to Lonrho.

He was succeeded as MP for Taunton by David Nicholson.

Ducking Stools

There were two ducking stools in Taunton in the 17th century. One was at Mill Pond at the top of the High Street and one was at Pool in North Town.

At first it was believed to have been used to punish those who used false weights and measures or for brewing bad ale. Women were more likely to be involved in these activities and, therefore, more likely to be punished by 'cooking' or 'ducking'. Later on other offences became the subject of this type of punishment, including 'brawlers and scolders' and prostitutes. Initially it does not appear that the chair was used for ducking but that the recipient of the punishment was strapped in and put on show in a similar way to those who were punished in the stocks. Ducking under water came later and typically involved ducking beneath the water three times.

Toulmin in his book on Taunton, writing in 1791, says that he can remember the ducking stool being used 'Within the last fifty years for ducking disorderly and scolding women.' It is believed that Bettie Wyatt of North Town was the last woman to suffer this punishment in Taunton.

The Eastgate

The east gate was probably the most important entrance to the town in medieval times. It was positioned at the top of the slope looking over East Reach. The first known mention of its existence was in 1158. Originally access would have been controlled by means of a wooden pole but it is likely that a medieval masonry gateway was constructed at a later date before being destroyed, probably in the Civil War. Until 1817 the street narrowed at this point and there was a building in the middle.

Evacuation

Already on the 2 September 1939, the day before Britain and France declared war on Germany the newspapers were reporting the imminent arrival of evacuees. It was given the name 'Operation Piper'. As well as taking a number of evacuees in their own right, Taunton was a focal point for receiving evacuees to be distributed to other areas. This was also the beginning of the blackout.

WEST SOMERSET IS READY

EVACUATED CHILDREN ARRIVING THIS WEEK-END

FULL PLANS FOR THE AREA

A.R.P. PLANS COMPLETED : LIST OF TAUNTON WARDENS

The Somerset County Herald of 2 September 1939 announces the forthcoming arrival of evacuees.

Those who took in evacuees were entitled to a billeting fee which was paid weekly.

Many of those who were evacuated in 1939 returned home when the expected bombing did not begin. A report in the Somerset County Herald of the 21 October stated that nearly half the evacuees to Taunton from London had returned home. In fact, 182 mothers and 303 children had returned home 'leaving 280 mothers and 488 children still in Taunton.'

However when the bombing did occur in August 1940 the authorities became overwhelmed by the sudden exodus of evacuees. In total, nearly 4,000 were evacuated to Taunton. In addition, Taunton acted as an important hub for organising evacuation to the surrounding towns and villages. Not all the evacuees were from London. For example, a consignment of four trains arrived from Hastings without warning. Even so, everyone was found a place within 48 hours.

The evacuation affected local schooling. It meant the addition of temporary schools and the 'sharing' of school time. In some cases whole schools were evacuated. This was the case with Coburn School which was evacuated from London. They shared Bishop Fox's School in Staplegrove Road. Bishop Fox's girls were taught in the morning and Coburn School in the afternoon. A new school had been built at Kingston Road and the Bishop Fox's girls were able to move there in the Spring of 1940.

Fiennes, Celia (1662 - 1741)

Celia Fiennes was a contemporary of Daniel Defoe. She lived near Salisbury and was the daughter of a colonel in Cromwell's army. She travelled for her health and for adventure and visited every county in England.

She wrote her travel memoirs in 1702 but it was not published until 1888 under the title *Through England on a Side Saddle.* The following extract is from her tour of 1698 from Bristol to Plymouth:

Monument to Celia Fiennes in 'No Man's Heath, Cheshire Photo, R Haworth

'*From thence to Taunton 16 miles through many small places and scattering houses, through lanes full of stones and by the great rains just before full of wet and dirt. It passed over a large common or bottom of deep black land which is bad for the rider but good for the abider as the proverb is; this was 2 or 3 mile long and pass'd and repass'd a river as it twin's about at least ten tymes over stone bridges. This river comes from Bridge water 7 mile, the tyde comes up beyond Bridge water, even within 3 miles of Taunton its flowed by the tide which brings up the barges with coal to this place, after having pass'd a large common which on either hands leads a greta waye, good rich land with ditches and willow trees all for feeding cattle, and here at this little place where the boates unlade the coale ye packhorses comes and takes it in sacks and so carryes it to ye places all about. This is ye sea coale brought from Bristol, the horses carry 2 bushell at a tyme wich at the place cost 18d and when its brought to Taunton cost 2 shillings. The roads were full of these Carryers going and returning.*

Taunton is a large town having houses of all sorts of buildings both brick and stone, but mostly timber and plaister, its a very neate place and looks substantial as a place of good trade. You meete all sorts of country women wrapp'e up in the mantles calle West Country rockets, a large mantle doubled together of a sort of serge, some are Linsywolsey and a deep fringe or ffag at the lower end, these hang down some to their feete some only just below ye wast, in the summer they are all in white garments of this sort, in the winter they are in red ones. I call them garments because they never go out without them and this is the universal ffashion in Somerset and Devonshire and Cornwall. Here is a good market cross well carv'd and a large market house on pillars for the corn. I was in the largest Church, it was mending, it was pretty large, the alter stood table wayes in the middle of the chancell, there was one good stone statue stood in the wall, the effigee was very tall in a ruff and long black dress like some religious with his gloves and book in his hand. There were several little monuments with inscriptions round them, they have encompass'd the church yard with a new brick wall and handsom iron gates, there is a large space called the Castle yard and some remains of the Castle walls and buildings which is fitted up for a good dwelling house. '

Finch, William

William Finch was made the Suffragan Bishop in 1538 by Henry VIII. When he died, no further bishop was nominated until the Rt. Rev, Charles Fane de Sallis in 1911. The Bishop of Taunton is suffragan, or assistant, to the Bishop of Bath and Wells.

Floods

In 1960 Taunton suffered severe flooding. The flooding most severely affected Station Road where 360 houses and business premises were flooded with damage estimated at £114,000. The surrounding villages of Bathpool, Ruishton and Creech St Michael were also particularly badly affected. At the time the authorities stated that rainfall of such a magnitude could only be expected once every 70 years, However, only six years later it was to happen again.

In 1968 the town centre was saved form a repeat performance by the River Tone Improvement Scheme which was instituted following the flooding in 1960. Although not completed in 1968, it was sufficiently ad-

A lorry from Colthurst Timber Yard caught in the 1960 floods.

vanced to contain much of the water. Under the scheme, the river channel, which was narrow and had a number of bends, was widened and straightened.

However, despite these improvements, Musgrove Hospital lost its power supply for a short while. Ambulance men came to their aid using vehicle batteries for emergency lighting.

In the 1980's, the flood walls and embankments on the Tone were updated to give additional protection.

On 27 October 2000 there was a special flood awareness day 40 years after the great flood of 1960. Three days later the water came to within inches of breaching the bridge and flowing into Bridge Street and North Street. The improved flood defences worked but it was touch and go. Hundreds of sandbags were issued to homes and businesses by the local council. Traffic was barred from the town centre and many businesses remained closed

Other significant years of flood were 1810, 1875, 1882, 1889,1894,1929,1994 and 1995. In 2007 Taunton avoided the serious flooding that occurred in neighbouring Gloucester and other parts of the country.

Flower Show

The flower show began life on 16th August 1866.

Taunton Flower Show

Its antecedents lay in the founding of the Taunton and West Somerset Horticultural Society in 1831, under the auspices of John Young who had nurseries in what is now the Elms Estate off Staplegrove Road. In 1894 the Borough Council purchased land adjacent to Wilton House owned by the Kinglake family and established Vivary Park.

Over the years the Flower Show has grown in stature earning itself the epithet, 'Chelsea of the West.'

Though it survived two world wars, in 1997 a flash flood resulted in the site being covered in two feet of water. The public were barred from entry while the judges carried out their task in waders.

In 2008 Taunton won the national title for Britain in Bloom in the large town/ small city category, for the first time. Organised by the Royal Horticultural Society, it is the largest competition of its kind in Europe.

French Weir

The history of French Weir can be traced back to the 13th century when it was known as Frenswer.

It was built to drive a fulling mill, to clean and thicken cloth, and for a corn mill in the area that is now Goodlands Gardens.

In 1793 the weir was destroyed by an army of women who believed the town miller was sending flour out from the town in a time of food shortages.

Over the years it became a popular spot for bathing. In 1813 the Taunton

Society for the Preservation of Peace announced their intention of prosecuting those who chose to bathe naked. However, its popularity as a place to bathe continued and in 1862 a bathing station was constructed and bathing charged at 2d a time. In 1864 the first annual swimming and diving match took place, though once again it caused controversy as the male contestants took part in the nude.

In 1838 an extension to the Grand Western Canal was opened at French Weir only to be closed in 1867 after the coming of the railway and its purchase by the Bristol and Exeter Railway.

In 1910 the dilapidated condition of part of the retaining walls and the foundations of the weir resulted in the leakage of water such that the mill owners, who still operated at that time, claimed compensation for loss of water. A new weir was constructed.

The Horse Chestnut trees that are so characteristic of the park are over a 100 years old. They were planted in 1898.

A curiosity was the positioning of a tank there in 1919 to mark the achievement of raising nearly £3 million in war savings. It remained there until it was sold as scrap in 1939.

Frier, Harry (1849-1921)

Harry Frier, working in the 19th century, produced between two and three thousand paintings, a good number of which were of Taunton and the surrounding areas. They are an valuable record of Taunton at this time.

Born Henry in Edinburgh on 2 May 1849, he soon became known as Harry. His father, Robert, was the owner of a successful drapery and clothing business who, in later life, sold his business in order to make painting his profession. All the children were encouraged to paint and draw. After leaving school, Harry successfully passed his entrance exam to Edinburgh School of Art and enrolled on a three year course.

After finishing his course in 1870 he taught part-time at George W. Watson's College in Edinburgh. He moved to London in the midst of the 'Great Depression' in 1878. There was little money for art except among the wealthy and his reputation was not well enough established. He failed to make a success in London but did meet his future wife, Kezia Catherine Dyer (known as Kate) while employed as a scene painter in a London Music Hall. She was one of the chorus girls.

After they fell in love in 1879, they visited Somerset for the first time to visit her mother at Creech St Michael. When they visited Harry's parents in Edinburgh, however, Kate was not welcomed. It appears that they did not like the thought of him marrying a lower class girl. It is believed that he did not meet his parents again after that visit.

They were married in Taunton Registry Office on 1 March 1881 and settled permanently in Taunton in 1883, living in Hyde Lane, Bathpool to begin with, either with Kate's mother or in the adjacent cottage. The marriage of a middle class painter to a working class girl would have been considered unusual at this time.

He rented a studio above a millinery shop at 5a East Reach and began working in oils. Though he had one or two early commissions, they were time consuming and not very profitable. Instead he turned to painting houses and views, approaching the owners of larger properties with a view to commissioning a painting.

Though some of his works appear accomplished, others appeared amateurish in their execution. He had a relaxed attitude which seemed to influence his work and was never able to do more than just make ends meet. Due to lack of money he gave up his studio in East Reach in 1891 and moved to 11 Greenbrook Terrace. He sold watercolour drawings at Alfred Vickery's artist materials shop at 16 Bridge Street and in 1893 he became friendly with William Corbett, a photographer at 26 Bath Place and began producing monochrome watercolours in imitation of photographic prints.

In 1894 Kate suffered an eye injury. Though she regained her sight, she did not completely recover and her eye had the appearance of being permanently half-closed. Harry, too, had poor vision in one eye.

Charles Tite

The relationship between Harry and Kate was never harmonious and deteriorated over the years. Harry wanted children but they were to remain childless. Kate did not receive the security of income from Harry that she may have expected.

The period between 1895 and 1905 was when he produced his best work. They moved to Bath Place in 1895 though they returned to Greenbrook Terrace within two years (this time to number 15), probably because Bath Place proved too expensive.

He formed a beneficial association with Charles Tite, secretary and later Vice President of the

Natural History Society, who formed a collection of over 6,000 books and prints of Somerset. He paid Harry to produce sketches of local scenes and characters and allowed him to sell copies on.

In 1898 Harry designed the largest proscenium and backcloth ever erected in Taunton for a romantic opera called 'In the Days of the Siege.', set in Taunton during the civil war.

He began to feel the effect of competition from the new picture postcards which were much cheaper than his topographic watercolours and after 1890 he found it more and more difficult to make money. He hawked his pictures around public houses and began to drink too much. His relationship with Kate worsened and his work declined. They often settled bills with paintings and, increasingly, he confined himself to his room upstairs in the house. He took on an 18 year old pupil who paid 5s a visit and in 1911 took on further pupils. His drinking increased. Sometimes he would be so drunk he would wander into the wrong house on the way back from the pub.

In 1912, at the age of 63, Kate caught bronchitis and died. Harry was inconsolable, despite their difficult relationship. After her death he stopped taking pupils and became a recluse.

Kate's niece, Lottie, took pity on him and took him into her house in 1914 when he was 65 but his behaviour became intolerable and in April 1917 he entered the Poor Law Institution in Trinity Street, formerly the workhouse He hated the regime and after six weeks he was once again with his niece. He stayed with her for a few months before he entered the workhouse again. Eventually he discharged himself and lodged at the District Nurse's house in Paul Street. Charles Tite helped him once more with a 7s a week pension. In 1919 he was evicted from his lodgings and moved back into the workhouse. By now he was suffering from senile dementia. He died in the workhouse on Saturday 19 February 1921.

There was no money to pay for his funeral at the churchyard at Creech St Michael.

In his obituary in the Somerset County Gazette, Charles Tite wrote prophetically, 'Tauntonians of the future will owe Mr Frier a debt of gratitude for having preserved for them the sketches of many of the old buildings in Taunton which have now been demolished.'

Paitning by Harry Friar of the New Inn, Wilton, 1898. This is now the Vivary Arms.
Picture by Harry Frier SANHS

Gerard, Thomas

In his survey of West Somersetshire in 1633 he says, 'The climate, particularly of that part which is called the *Vale of Taunton Dean*, is peculiarly mild and serene; and the soil highly fertile and productive. The eye is agreeably relieved by a judicious mixture of arable and pasture; and if it be contrasted with some parts of the Northern district, it may emphatically be called the land of *Canaan.*'

The Glorious Revolution

During the Glorious Revolution (or the Revolution of 1688), King James II of England (VII of Scotland) was overthrown by an alliance of Parliamentarians and an invasion from Holland by an army led by William of Orange, who became William III of England.

William of Orange, William III of Engalnd , aged 27

Though this was an invasion by a foreign army it marked the establishment of a constitutional monarchy. It limited the powers of the monarch in many important respects and he or she became subject to the will of parliament.

It also was to mark the end of the re-establishment of Catholicism. Catholics were denied the right to vote and sit in parliament and the monarch was forbidden to marry a Catholic or be a Catholic. Limited rights were granted to non-conformists.

With Taunton's history of dissent, its support for parliament during the Civil War and, more recently, for the Duke of Monmouth, and the persecution that had resulted, it was no wonder that the Glorious Revolution was welcomed in Taunton.

An address was sent to the new King from the Justices of the Peace and the Grand Jury to assure the King that the people of Somerset were 'as warmly devoted to your service, as the most zealous of all your dominions.' It went on, 'It has indeed been our misfortune to be very ill represented in parliament; but we have still been untainted in our own breasts. We have been overpowered, but not corrupted' A further declaration of support was made and 'signed by all the justices, except one, and by every one of the grand jury.'

Edward Goldsworthy (1817-1896)

Edward Goldsworthy's 'pamphlet', published in 1883, is an important record of events in the early part of the nineteenth century.

His purpose, he recollects, was 'to show the condition of the streets of Taunton, and the habits of the people fifty or sixty years ago.'

SANHS

Only the central parts of Taunton were paved, he notes. Silver Street was an immoral place, noted for the residence of a class known as the 'great social evil'. This was also where the theatre was. Most of the comedians lodged in the courts and the alleys of East Reach. He remembered as a boy watching the actor Charles Keane (son of the great Edmund Keane) act in either Othello or Richard III.

There was no Alma Street in those early years of the 19th century. South Street was known as Holway Lane. There was horse racing and balloon launching from the area off South Road where King's College was later built. The race days were big events, 'general holidays for all classes.' He recounts how at the races he saw a thief steal a silver tankard which he passed onto an accomplice. Then the thief was captured. He recalls, 'He frightened me out of my senses by telling me I was about to swear to what might hang him .....I thought it was all so dreadful that I said I was not quite sure that he was the thief.'

From Shuttern you could walk down the steps to the river. There was no Haines Hill or yet the Weslyan College (later to become Queens College). There were only three houses between Cann Street and Bishop's Hull. North Town had only a handful of houses and was dominated by Yarde House inhabited by Miss Halliday, the 'Lady of North Town' , who kept a rookery, 'which prevented people from sleeping.' Flooding of the road near North Town Bridge was a regular occurrence resulting in a central arch being built.

East Street was a great thoroughfare from London to Exeter and was the centre of business of the town. This was before the coming of the railway. 'The arrival and departure of the North Devon and Bridport Mails, and other coaches, was the great event of the day.' Travelling to Bristol or Exeter was a major undertaking 'and a journey to London made a man an oracle for life.'

Houses with a 'half door' were the order of the day, 'part of which the old people were often seen leaning over and chatting with friends.'

Bath Place was known as Hunt's Court, 'a rough and dirty court, having only a narrow strip of pavement in the middle.' The Four Alls public house which has only changed its name in recent years (now the Rajpoot Indian Restaurant) was already there. A good lot of the Sedan Chair carriers lived in Hunt's Court, 'as drunken a lot of men as any in the town.' The Sedan Chair was 'a sort of upright box, with a top to lift up and down, a glass door in front, and long moveable poles at the side, the sound made by these chairs, when in motion, was a very peculiar flapping sound, and could be heard a long way off.'

Rows of butchers and a fish market stood in and around the Parade and 'it was not an uncommon thing to see a fish women quarrelling within hearing of their worships'. Hammet Street had not changed in appearance much. He recounts the details of the building of the new tower at St Mary's Church, costing £4,002 5s 5d. Tangier was a field known as 'Rats Island'. The proprietress of the Castle Inn was a Mrs Sweet. He remembers from close quarters as a boy seeing the arrival of Donna Maria, Queen of Portugal. The bridge at the junction of North Street and Bridge Street 'was fifty years ago the liveliest part of the town as coal and goods were brought by water and uploaded there.' About a hundred people were employed in this business and were some of the roughest and coarsest lot in the whole town.' Fights were frequent. Floods were a regular feature here too, and it was common at times of flood to be ferried across to the bridge.

In Fore Street was a Chandler's shop where candles and soap were manufactured which 'on melting days was so sickening that people were obliged to shut their doors and windows, and stop their noses.' It was only surpassed by a similar operation in East Street.

He regrets the passing of two clear streams running from Eastgate to the bottom of North Street and from the top of the High Street to the bottom of North Street. He remembers the opening of the Bridgwater to Tiverton Canal, a day of sleet, snow and rain, 'intended to be a gay day, but there was not a bit of gaiety or cheerfulness about the whole affair.'

The area around Cann Street, like Silver Street, was a rough area. In a lane off Cann Street was 'The Black Boy Inn', kept by Anthony Jarrett, who had been acquitted of murdering a soldier and throwing him over the bridge. 'Vice and drunkenness reigned throughout this neighbourhood. It was known as the "sink of iniquity". It was such a worry to the Taunton of the day that at the instigation of the Mayor, Peter Taylor, the houses were pulled down and the residents given compensation.

He also recounts how real a fear there was of body snatchers. He remembers how, when his brother died, his father and mother were afraid that his body would be taken from the grave, so much so that 'it became my duty to examine the grave daily and to report that all was right and undisturbed.'

He comments on the poor state of education at that time, 'The present generation', he laments, 'will scarcely believe what ignorance existed sixty years ago.' He recounts his own education at Crockford School in Church Square, 'where I received abundance of caning but little instruction.'

He praises the improvement in health which he believes was mainly due to the introduction of the Board of Health and better drainage and "All classes are more cleanly in their habits.', so that the town is now 'rarely visited by epidemics.' In these earlier times 'both rich and poor lived surrounded with dirt and bad smells. The poor generally had a horror of soap and water, and the rich were not very fond of it.'

He makes some interesting comments about the results of the introduction of gas lighting 'when things seemed to go on faster and people grew sharper.' There was also the emergence of steam which had ' changed the mode of conducting business, and offered facilities for travelling and gaining knowledge which our forefathers did not possess and the addition of the telegraph has revolutionised everything.'

Letters from London cost eight pence or ten pence, 'The letters of the poor often remained at the Post Office for several days.... before they could get the money to pay for them.'

Popular pastimes were often of a cruel and violent nature. They included bull-baiting, cudgel playing, cock fighting and wrestling using hobnail boots (see seperate entries). He puts down some of the brutality to the return of the men from the Peninsula Wars which had 'brutalised men's feelings, and made them coarse minded and indifferent to blood and danger.'

Drinking habits were also a cause for concern. The rich liked 'Dining out drinking until they fell out of their chairs' and ' the lower classes imitated the rich but in a coarser manner.' The propensity for drink was nowhere more visible than in elections which in Taunton 'were a disgrace to all England.' Electors were bribed with barrels of beer.

The damp and dirty lock-up or 'Nook' was near the churchyard. It was 'infested with rats, and filthy in the extreme. Into this hold drunken and bleeding men were thrust.'

In general he has praise for the improvements made to the town. However he hopes that the Corporation ' will endeavour to supply the town with plenty of pure water and that "Winters" and "Poolwall" streams will again be allowed to flow and sparkle through the gutters of the streets as formerly.

Gordon, Charles George (1833-1885)

A British general, educated at Taunton School, who became a national hero for his exploits in China and his ill-fated defence of Khartoum against the Mahdi rebels.

Born in Woolwich, London, he was educated at Fullands School (closed in 1888) and Taunton

School. When he left Taunton School he went to the Royal Military Academy in Woolwich. He was commissioned into the Royal Engineers in 1852 and while serving at Pembroke Dock in Wales found his faith in Christ. This was to develop and inform many of his decisions over his career.

He then served in the Crimean War, was appointed Assistant Boundary Commissioner for the new Russian-Turkish boundary and took part in the Second Opium War. He stayed in China where he was appointed commander of the 'Ever Victorious Army.' He led them to a number of victories over the Taipings. Gordon resigned his command when the Manchus had the leader of the Taipings executed in his absence. He was persuaded to return but refused a bribe of 100,000 gold pieces from the Emperor. This further enhanced his reputation for incorruptibility and he earned the name 'Chinese Gordon'.

He held several important positions thereafter including the Governorship of Equatoria (1873-6) and as Governor-general of the Sudan between 1877-9 and 1884-5. During this time he was praised for his efforts to halt the slave trade. He was sent to Khartoum when the Mahdi revolted in 1884 with no clear instructions of how to proceed. He organised the evacuation of 2,600 soldiers and civilians before the city was surrounded. The relief expedition took a long time to organise. When it eventually reached Khartoum on 28 January 1885 it found the city already captured and Gordon dead for two days (just before his 52nd birthday). There was a great outpouring of public grief at home and an intense criticism of Gladstone's administration which threatened to bring down the government.

Hamilton, Mary

One of the strangest cases that came before the quarter sessions at Taunton must have been that of Mary Hamilton who was charged in February 1746 with pretending to be a man and marrying 14 wives. She used two male aliases, George and Charles. Mary Price, the last of his 'wives' condemned 'his vile and deceitful practices', believing for the first three months that she was indeed married to a man. She was sentenced to be whipped as a cheat through four towns.

Hammett, Benjamin (1737- 1800)

The son of a serge-maker, he began his career as a porter for a London bookseller. He later became a successful London banker. He built Wilton House, became an alderman and was Member of Parliament for Taunton from 1790 and his death in 1800.

He purchased the offices of Keeper of the Castle and Bailiff of the Manor for his sons and nephew E. J. Esdaile in 1786 following the death of the heiress of the Lucas family in 1785, and used his money to ensure he kept his seat as a Member of Parliament. He was responsible for the restoration of the castle and, when funds raised by public subscription to repair the Assize Hall fell short, he put in £218 9s 4d. The other sitting member, Alexander Popham, contributed £105, while £94 was contributed from other subscribers.

Hammet Street

His most obvious legacy was the building of Hammet Street in 1788. He was able to demolish the existing houses by an Act of Parliament. He was knighted by George III in 1786.

Hestercombe Gardens

Only 3 miles from the centre of Taunton on the southern slopes of the Quantocks, Hestercombe Gardens is three fine gardens in one. Yet it is only in recent years that their worth has been fully appreciated.

The Georgian Landscaped garden in the valley to the north of Hestercombe was created between 1750 and 1856 by Copplestone Warre Bampfylde.

The Victorian Terrace at the southern end, adjacent to the

Part of the formal gardens at Hestercombe

Edwardian Garden, was created by Viscount Portman who acquired the house and gardens after the death of Elizabeth, the last of the Warre's, in 1872. At the same time he modified the house.

His grandson, Edward, commissioned a new formal garden beyond the Victorian Terrace in 1903. Created by Edward Lutyens and planted by Gertrude Jekyl between 1904 and 1908, it is considered the finest example of their work together. However, it was so nearly lost to a scheme to cover it in Tarmac to provide parking for the Devon and Somerset Fire Service. There was an outcry when this was proposed in 1973 and the scheme was rejected, but only by a single vote.

In 1992, a local man, Philip White, 're-discovered' the garden and due to his vision and determination resulting in the creation of the Hestercombe Gardens Project in 1995, the restoration of the garden was begun. In 2003 the Hestercombe Gardens Trust was created to protect the gardens for the future and to manage the three gardens.

During the war Hestercombe was the rear Headquarters of the 8th Corps, responsible for British troops and defence in Somerset, Devon, Cornwall and Bristol. The main headquarters was based at Pyrland Hall.

It was split into 'A' Branch, the Adjutants's Branch and 'Q' Branch, the Quartermaster's Branch. About 200 personnel were based there. The basement housed the telephone exchange and the 'Battle HQ' in case of an invasion.

The operation expanded in 1941 with the building of six barrack blocks.

The 8th Corps left Hestercombe in January 1943 to accompany the Allied Invasion Forces of the 21st Army Group. Many of them subsequently became part of the Allied offensive in Africa.

8th Corps at Pyrland Hall became HQ of South West District and Hestercombe became the HQ of the 19th district US supply services. More barracks and nissen huts were built (Only one building of the war period survives today).

General Eisenhower visited Hestercombe in the company of General Gerow, who was based at Norton Camp, on 19 March 1944.

The administrative staff were privy to the invasion date for D-Day and six weeks before were confined to barracks under guard.

After D-Day, 6 June 1944, the staff were ordered to Cherbourg.

On 16 May 1941 at five minutes after midnight a Junckers JU 88 crashed in the drive of Hestercombe House. The pilot, Lieutenant Freidrich Kerkoff, was trapped in the burning aircraft while the other three members of the crew were able to para-

Junkers 88 similar to that shot down at Hestercombe

chute to safety. Kerkoff died and was later buried at the German Military Cemetery at Cannock Chase in Staffordshire. It was shot down by canon fire from a mosquito of number 218 squadron piloted by Squadron Leader H. V. Ellis and Flight Lieutenant J. M. Craig.

Hill, Roger of Poundsford

A wealthy lawyer who was granted the Castle after it had been taken away from the Bishop of Winchester in 1648. He refused to allow the assizes to be held there as they had been formerly until 1656 when he agreed on condition that a sum of 10s a year was paid. With the restoration his right to the Castle was taken away from him. He paid the headmaster's salary for the grammar school in the Old Municipal Building for 12 years.

Holy Trinity Church

Established in June 1842 off East Reach to serve a growing population largely as a result of the expansion caused by the railways. Its first vicar was the Revd F. J. Smith. It has a tower nearly 90 feet tall and is built of white lias stone, built by local architect Richard Carver. It cost £5,000 to build. There have been a number of alterations and additions since the building of the church including a new vestry built at the turn of the twentieth century, a Lady Chapel built after the First World War and, at the end of the twentieth century, a further chapel in memorium.

Home Guard

The 2nd Somerset (Taunton) Battalion was formed in May 1940 under Major L. A. Jones. It covered the whole of Taunton Deane plus Chard and Ilminster, though by April 1943 a seperate Ilminster Battalion had been formed. In total it comprised about 2,000 men. The Taunton Compa-

Image from the cover of the Home Guard Manual

nies were Taunton North, Taunton South, Taunton (Great Western Railway), Bishop's Lydeard, Blagdon Hill, Wellington and Stoke St Mary.

In the early days there were only 200 rifles for the whole of Somerset. An appeal was made for any sort of gun or rifle and in the absence of these, axes, pitchforks, sticks and the like were used. However, by the end of July 1940 a million Springfield rifles had been shipped from America and uniforms had been supplied.

No members of the 2nd Battalion were known to have lost their lives during action during the war. However, they had an important strategic role in case of invasion. As part of the lead up to 'D-Day', 'A' and 'C' Company of the Home Guard were instructed to protect White Ball Tunnel and 'B' Company the bridge at Norton Fitzwarren and the Cogload Flyover. These companies were linked by telephone with Langport Home Guard who were guarding the tunnel at Somerton. At some point it appears there was a case of sabotage when it was discovered that the telephone wires between the Langport Home Guard and 'A' and 'C' Companies had been cut.

To the surprise of many people, the Home Guard was told that it was no longer required in a broadcast by the Secretary of State of War, Sir James Grigg, on 6 September 1944. By early December they had all stood down.

Hospital

The first plans for a hospital, off present day South Road, were drawn up in 1770 and in 1772. The Prime Minister, Lord North, laid the foundation stone. It was never completed, though, through lack of money and was sold as a private house which became known as The Lodge. Later it was to become a convent.

The first Taunton hospital, which was abandoned through lack of money.

The East Reach Hospital opened in 1812 at the instigation of Dr Malachi Blake, to coincide with George III's jubilee. It could accommodate 26 people. By 1842 east and west wings had been added costing £2,765 and, with further extensions in 1872, the capacity was increased to 100. In 1888, this time to celebrate Queen Victoria's Jubilee, a nursing institute, was built next to the hospital. The money was raised by an appeal from Dr Edward Liddon and Dr William Kelly. They kicked off the appeal by donating £1,000 and were greatly helped by an individual donation of £5,000 by James Broadbent of Langport.

Trinity Hospital was established at the site of the Union Workhouse. It was taken over by the Ministry of Health in 1948.

An Eye Infirmary was established in 1816 in North Street by James Billet (after which Billet Street is named). It moved to Upper High Street in 1845 and then to Shuttern at the site of the Turnpike House in Shuttern. It closed in 1904.

The site of East Reach Hospital and to the right, the Nursing Institute

Taunton: An A - Z

There were three mental asylums at various times in the 19th century in Taunton at Fulland's House, Fairwater (absorbed by Taunton School) and Amber House (Trull), before the establishment of Tone Vale Hospital in 1897 and Sandhill Park (for mentally ill children) in 1925. Sandhill Park was requisitioned by the military to become the 41st General Military Hospital in August 1940. From 1941 it was leased to the Americans as a neurological hospital and remained in military use until 1944. It reopened in 1948 under the National Health Service and some new buildings were constructed. The hospital site was sold, partly for housing in 1991. With the advent of the policy of care in the community, Tone Vale Hospital was closed in 1995 and the site was given over to the building of a new village taking the old name of Cotford St Luke.

Musgrove Hospital had its origins in the war. It was built by the American army in 1942 as the 67th General Hospital. It was one of seven war hospitals in the Taunton area. As well as the above mentioned Sandhill Park military hospital (185th) there were also hospitals at Norton Camp (101st) and at Hestercombe House (801st).

Musgrove Hospital continued in use as a Ministry of Pensions Hospital before becoming a general hospital within the National Health Service in 1951.

The following information is taken from the Taunton & Somerset Trust figures for 2007.

Musgrove Hospital, which had its roots in the Second World War.

It serves a population of 340,000. Each year over 40,000 patients are admitted as emergencies; 10,000 patients are admitted for elective surgery; 28,000 are seen for day-care surgery; 197,000 patients attend outpatient clinics; 45,000 attended Accident and Emergency. In addition, 3,000 babies are born in the maternity department and 170,000 diagnostic tests are carried out each year. There are 700 beds and 15 operating theatres. The annual budget is £180 million and over 4,000 staff are employed.

Hydrographic Office

The Hydrographic Office has been charting the world's oceans for over 200 years.

The Admiralty's Hydrographic Department was established in 1795 By Earl Spencer, the same year that saw the compulsory introduction of lemon juice to prevent scurvy on board ship. The first chart was issued by Alexander Dalrymple in 1801, an employee of the East India Company. From 1819 permission was given to sell charts to the Merchant Navy. The department at that time consisted of the hydrographer, an assistant and a draughtsman.

Rear Admiral Sir Francis Beaufort

The service was developed greatly under the tireless efforts of the fourth hydrographer, Rear Admiral Sir Francis Beaufort, inventor of the Beaufort Scale in 1805 to estimate wind speeds and their effects. He served between 1829 and 1855. He expanded coverage all over the world so that by 1855 there were 1,981 charts listed within the chart catalogue.

The coverage was further developed in the latter part of the 19th century and into the twentieth century, spurred on by the development of the Echo Sounder and Sonar. Now over 1,000 people are employed in the UK Hydrographic Office at Admiralty Way, Taunton.

Approval for a site in Taunton was granted as early as 1938. At that time, the production of charts through their various stages was spread over a number of sites which did not make for an efficient or speedy operation. The reason that Taunton was chosen as an integrated site was that it was not considered a prime target for bombing and that it had good transport links with the important naval bases of Plymouth and Portsmouth.

A piece of land was purchased which was large enough to allow for future expansion though due to the advent of the war a move was delayed. By June 1941 a good deal of the printing and reproduction side had been moved to Taunton.

Through 1944 and 1945, the offices at Taunton and Bath worked under great pressure to publish the essential surveys being made at that time in Northern Europe. Without their efforts the D-Day Landing may not have taken place.

It was not until 1968 that the integration of the Hydrographic Office under one department was complete. Approval for a cartography building was given in 1963 and work started in 1964. Work on the building fell behind schedule. The Chief Hydrographer of the time, Admiral Ritchie, announced that the move would take place in April 1968, whether the building was ready or not. On the 16 April the first occupants moved in. The newcomers were welcomed as 'instant citizens' by the Mayor of Taunton.

The move to Taunton was followed by the introduction of modern printing machinery and computers for drafting and cartography. Metrication was introduced in 1967, though it took longer to implement than first envisaged.

Today, digital and web-based products complement the admiralty paper charts and publications. In February 2005 the UK Hydrographic Office attracted worldwide attention when it published detailed pictures of the In-

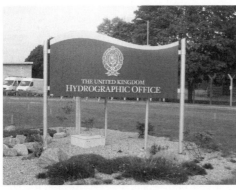

dian Ocean floor in the area where the tsunami disaster of 26 December 2004 took place.

As of 2008, the UK Hydrographic site at Taunton is to be completely redeveloped and will remain on its current site after months of speculation that it might be move elsewhere.

Ina, King

King of Wessex between 688 and 726. He created some form of settlement in Taunton though its exact whereabouts are unknown. There is evidence that he granted land next to the Tone and beyond to Beorthwald, the Abbot of Glastonbury. Taunton was destroyed in 1722 according to The Anglo Saxon Chronicle by his Queen, Ethelburg, possibly because of a quarrel or to prevent its use as a fortification by rebels.

Jeboult, Edward (1829-1893)

We owe much to Edward Jeboult in our understanding of Taunton in Victorian times. As well as publishing a history of Taunton, he wrote an unpublished eleven volume work on Taunton and his family. In 1981 Robin Bush 'discovered' two of the volumes.

He was born in 1829, the third son of James and Harriett. He was educated at home until he was nearly 10. He went to two schools in Taunton before entering the Wellington Academy where he became Head Boy and excelled at sport.

He left school at 16 and became apprenticed to a builder. Following the death of his brother, William, in April 1850, he became the manager of the drapers his father had purchased for William just before his death. He made a success of it and sold it in 1854. He then became employed as a Clerk of Works for the Taunton and West of England Patent Manure Company and then in a similar capacity for J. H. Beadon for work at Kingston House. In 1855 he became a builder in his own right and by 1857 had 60 people working for him. After two unsuccessful courtships he married Henrietta Summerhayes at Saint Mary's Church on 11 June 1863. He was 33 while she was only 20. They had 12 children together, two dying in infancy, one at the age of nine.

He gave up the building business feeling that there was not enough profit in it and opened an ironmongers at 40 North Street in 1864. It was a large shop, 200 feet long. In 1868 he became temporary surveyor to the Taunton Turnpike Trust. He took another shop at 48 High Street and a marble mason's yard in the High Street in 1870. In 1877 he moved to a new shop and workshop in Station Road calling it the West of England Stone and Marble Works. It specialised in rustic garden furniture.

It is thought that he was introduced to photography by his friend John Blizzard who set up in partnership with John Webber in 1864, giving up his job as schoolmaster. Jeboult took photographs as early as 1860 and he was soon offering to send free photographs of his stock.

In 1866 he felt ready to publish his first history of Taunton. He was to dedicate it to Lord Taunton but he delayed until 1873 as he wished to add sections on West Somerset and the Tone Valley. Only 100 of the 350 pages related to Taunton.

In 1890 he began to suffer a debilitating spinal condition. He died on 17 June 1893, aged 61. The second edition of his book on Taunton was published posthumously.

Jellalabad

The Jellalabad barracks were built in Mount Street in 1880 for the Somerset Light Infantry. The name was chosen as a result of the heroics of the Somerset Regiment at Jellalabad in Afghanistan amidst an otherwise disastrous campaign.

The Keep of the Jellalabad Barracks

The British had colonised India in the early 19th century via the Honourable East India Company and were obsessed by the notion of a Russian invasion via Afghanistan. When they launched a campaign in Afghanistan in 1838 and installed a puppet regime under Shuja Shah, though, it was short-lived, and resulted in a humiliating retreat from Kabul and, in January 1842, the massacre of the garrison at Kabul under the command of Major-General William Elphinstone.

In November 1841, the Somerset Regiment and the 35th Bengal Army and a group of sappers under Brigadier Sir Robert Sale, were besieged at Jellalabad, about 80 miles east of Kabul. The sappers, under the direction of Captain George Broadfoot, set about rebuilding the defences which were in a terrible state. The Afghans surrounded the town but were pushed back by a sortie of the 35th Bengal Army under Colonel Dennie. On the 13 January, the sole survivor of the abandoned garrison at Kabul, Dr Brydon, reached Jellalabad, wounded and in a state of collapse. About the same time they were also told that there was to be no imminent relief of the Jellalabad garrison. The puppet Ameer in Kabul, Shah Shuja, sent several demands that they should abandon Jellalabad and withdraw to India.

There was a disagreement over what was to be done in the circumstances. Brigadier Sale and his chief of staff were for leaving, Captain's Oldfield and Havelock for staying. In the end the captain's had their way. If things were not bad enough, on 19 February an earthquake destroyed much of the fortifications. Once again, however, under the direction of Captain Broadfoot, the fortifications were restored. On 11 March there was another sortie under captain Dennie and 300 or so sheep were captured to help feed the garrison. On the 7 April three columns advanced from the garrison and attacked the Afghan forces under the command of Akbar Khan. There were, approximately, 1,500 men against 5,000-6,000 Afghans. They captured Akbar's artillery and drove his soldiers away and by the morning of the 8 of April the Afghan forces had fled. When they were finally relieved on 13 April by Captain Pollock's Army of Retribution, they were accompanied by the song, 'Oh, but you've been a long time coming.'

As a reward Queen Victoria ordered the regiment to be known as Prince Albert's Regiment of Light Infantry, the uniform was upgraded to reflect this and a special campaign medal was struck to commemorate the siege.

The imposing keep of the Jellalabad Barracks still remains. The barracks have been demolished and housing built in its place.

Jellalabad day is celebrated on the 7 April.

Kensit, John

Protestant agitator and founder of the Protestant Truth Society formed 'to oppose popery in the Church of England.' Along with his followers (the Kensites), he launched an attack on the established church in the High Street Temperance Hall in Taunton in 1901. However, the meeting ended in uproar and chairs were thrown about.

He died the following year in a great rally attended by thousands held in Birkenhead, Liverpool. It is claimed that he was murdered by a Catholic and that he was the last man in England to be martyred for the protestant cause.

Alexander Kinglake (1809-1891)

Born in Taunton on 5 August 1809, he was the author of a cult travel book and an eight volume definitive history of the Crimean War.

He was the second child and the eldest son of William Kinglake, banker and solicitor of Taunton, and Mary Woodforde. He went to Eton and Trinity College Cambridge and was called to the bar in 1837. In 1835, while still a student, he travelled throughout the east. This resulted in a travel book called *Eothen,* an account of his journey in the Levant. It came out in 1844 and

EOTHEN.

CHAPTER I.

OVER THE BORDER.

AT Semlin I still was encompassed by the scenes and the sounds of familiar life; the din of a busy world still vexed and cheered me; the unveiled faces of women still shone in the light of day. Yet, whenever I chose to look southward, I saw the Ottoman's fortress—austere, and darkly impending high over the vale of the Danube—historic Belgrade. I had come, as it were, to the end of this wheel-going Europe, and now my eyes would see the Splendour and Havoc of The East.

Opening paragraph of the cult novel, Eothen.

was an immediate success.

His interest in military affairs led him to travel to Algeria in 1845 to witness the French campaigns and to the Crimea in 1854. After Lord Raglan's death in 1856, Lady Raglan asked Kinglake to write a history of the Crimean War. This was his greatest achievement and it occupied much of the rest of his life. It was published in eight volumes between 1863 and 1887. The first two volumes were published in 1863 when he was 54. He did not complete them until 1887 when he was 78.

He lived mainly in London, for 20 years at Hyde Park Palace, where he knew Thackeray, Tennyson and Lord John Russell and a number of literary ladies of the day including Margaret Oliphant and Lucy Duff Gordon. He also lived for a time at Wilton House on the edge of Vivary Park in Taunton. He was MP for Bridgwater between 1857 and 1868 when he was unseated on charges of corruption perpetrated by his election agent.

His father, William, laid the first stone of the Crescent in 1807 and his brother, Dr Hamilton Kinglake was responsible for the copy of the ancient Market Cross in the Parade which was erected in 1867 and dedicated to both parents (The original market cross had been destroyed in 1771.) The Kinglake memorial was taken down in 1934. Land that was owned by the Kinglake family adjacent to Wilton House was purchased by the Borough Council in 1894 and used to establish Vivary Park.

Konigslutter

Taunton's twin town in Germany, population 17,000. Situated in lower Saxony in the district of Helmstedt on the Lutter stream.

Its origins are in the village of Lutter which is first mentioned in 1150. In 1200, the Duke of Braunschweig built a castle to the east of Lutter. The village developed into a small market town, receiving its first charter in around 1400. Seventy-three breweries were established. Mining and the cutting of limestone were also important industries.

In 1924, the surrounding villages of Oberlutter and Stiftlutter were incorporated into the town and in 1974 it grew further with the incorporation of a another 17 municipalities.

Lothar von Suepplingenberg, King and Emperor, founded the Benedictine Monastery and established the impressive St Peter and St Paul Church

Monastery Church in Konigslutter, Taunton's twin town in Germany

(or Emperor's Cathedral), as the monastic church in 1135. The west towers and the octagonal spire were added in the 15th century.

It has two museums: the Museum of Mechanical Musical Instruments and the Museum of Urban History.

In 2009, 25 years of twinning will be celebrated.

Law & Order

Early Prisons

The site of the Bridewell next to Tone Bridge

Apart from the Castle Prison (the Castle was regularly used for the Assizes and Quarter Sessions), there is evidence of a prison in the early years of the 14th century in the middle of the market (the modern parade) called the birdcage. It may have been used in a way more akin to the stocks to make an example of the occupant.

Two gaols called The Cow House and Little Ease were built beneath the Guildhall which was constructed in 1467 and in the last quarter of the 16th century the House of Correction or Bridewell was built next to Tone Bridge at the site of what was until recently the Singer Sewing Machine Shop. It was a forerunner of the workhouse giving employment to vagrants and the unemployed. However, over the years it became more and more to be used as a prison.

In the early years of the 17th century there were already complaints about the poor state of repair of the Bridewell. There are references to repairs in 1608 and 1612 and in 1650 the Court decided to grant £5 towards the repair.

In 1743 the gaoler, Nathaniel Gardiner, was accused of the murder of one of his female prisoners, Mary Ingham. He resisted arrest and tried to escape and had to be apprehended and dragged into his own prison. He must have escaped conviction, though, as his name is cited on later occasions where he was accused of violence or extortion towards his prisoners. The prison system encouraged corruption and extortion as until 1744 the gaoler received no remuneration from the state. He was expected to extract fees from the prisoners. An impoverished prisoner, therefore, who had no money to pay the gaolers fees may have stayed many months, or sometimes years, beyond his term until he could afford to pay off his debt.

In the 1777 edition of 'The State of the Prisons in England and Wales it is described how prisoners brought to Taunton from Ilchester Gaol infected the Court and beyond so that 'some hundreds died of the gaol distemper.'

Goldsworthy, writing in 1883 refers to the 'Nook' or lock-up which existed in his youth, situated near to St Mary's Church where 'drunken and bleeding men and women were thrust, and allowed to remain there until the following day.'

Wilton Gaol

In the Quarter Session held at Wells on 15 January 1754 the Court ordered that a new prison, 'a more convenient proper and commodious place' be built. A piece of land was purchased in Wilton for £300 on 3 October 1753. The completion of the new prison was announced in the Western Flying Post of 8 March 1756. The old gaol was put up for sale by auction. The prison was built in the shape of a church and was licensed to take up to 203 prisoners. There was an average of approximately 100 or so prisoners at any one time.

It was rebuilt and enlarged in 1815 to cover 4 acres of ground and its capacity increased to 275. It was enlarged again in 1843. The census return for 1851 shows that the population of actual prisoners in the gaol had increased to 154 from 121 in 1841.

In the seventh report of the inspectors of 1842, the inspector has no doubt of the causes of crime:

'It appears here that drunkenness is the most frequent cause of crime; nine out of ten of the prisoners have been in the habit of loitering about in public houses. Half of the letters which come from their wives allude to the bad company they formerly kept. Not one-seventh of the inmates are women; they are much better behaved in this county than in some parts. There is no doubt but that the beer shops have tended very much to increase crime. There were districts in this county from which few or no prisoners came until the existence of these beer-shops; they do immense mischief to the labourers.' Then he adds rather oddly. 'The best artisans here are said to be generally drunkards.'

The following pages show the diet book and the work schedule from the inspector's report of 1842 and gives a clue as to the severity of the regime. The treadmill which was an integral part of the work regime was installed in 1823 by Stothert and Pitt of Bath. It was used to grind corn which was then sold to the local bakers to make bread. A report made at the time by a local doctor is generally favourable.

'Dr Sully, of Wiveliscombe, having been applied to by high authority to deliver his sentiments on the effects of the treadmill, has visited Wilton Gaol, and has expressed his opinion that the exercise can in no way whatever affect the constitution of those employed there on - that the exercise, as a punishment, may be considered as very

The Police Station formerly Wilton Gaol

salutary and wholesome - and that it tends to keep the prisoners in good health and vigour. Dr Sully proposes the admission of air through ventilators, in front of the prisoners, above the wheel.'

During part of its existence a regime of silence was carried out within the prison.

The Ballad of Wilton Gaol

In 1868 a prisoner wrote a Christmas poem. It is 43 verses. The first six verses follow.

The Christmas bells are ringing out
Their Soul inspiring peals
And every one a Holy Joy
Within his bosom feels

The influence of the genial time
Makes all our hearts expand
To every creature on the earth
We stretch a friendly hand

With sunny smiles on every face
Content in everything
Nature herself appears to laugh
And Christmas carols sing

The young, the old, the rich, the poor
Unite with heart and voice
To celebrate their Christmas day
And bid us all rejoice

The sailor, on the ocean wide
Is carolling his strain
The soldier, in his barrack room
Or in the battle plain

The shepherd, on the mountain side
Pours forth his merry lay
And e'en the lonely lighthouse man
Remembers Christmas day

The gaol began to be leased to the military and by 1881 the majority of its prisoners emanated from the military.

In 1885 the gaol was handed over to the Somerset County Council and became the headquarters of the Somerset Constabulary. It remains in use as a police station today.

Police

The first police station was in Magdalene Street in 1840 at the site of St Mary's Poor House. A new station was built at the junction of the Crescent and Upper High Street in 1856. It was knocked down in 1963. The present Police Station, the former Wilton Gaol, is only a short distance away, on the opposite side of the road. It was rebuilt in 1943. The south wing was demolished and turned into a car park and the interior has been altered to accommodate a communications centre, a gym and a club for off-duty personnel.

Shire Hall

Erected to designs by William Moffat in the Elizabethan style. Consisting of an entrance hall, court rooms, retiring rooms, a Grand Jury and Judges lodgings as well as a number of cells in the basement. The foundation stone was laid by Viscount Portman in 1855. It opened in the spring of 1858 at a total cost of £28,000.

A Russian cannon captured during the Crimean War was given to the town in 1857 and was on display outside the Shire Hall for many years.

The 1874 Savage edition of Toulmin's History of Taunton describes a subterranean passage connecting it with Wilton Gaol.

The Shire Hall which opened in 1858

81. CLASSIFICATION AND LABOR TABLE FOR CONVICTED PRISONERS.

28, 29, Vic, c, 126, Sec. 19, 21, Sch. 1, Reg. 35, 36, 37, 38.

Hard Labor of 1st Class to consist of Tread Wheel, Crank, Shaft-Pump, Capstan, Stonebreaking, Flax Beating by Swingle and Flax Breaking by Crank, or Rope Beating, Oakum Picking as supplementary or non-effective Labor.

Hard Labor of 2nd Class to consist of Oakum or Rope Picking, Tailoring, Shoemaking, Mat Making, Weaving.

Employment for Criminal Prisoners not sentenced to Hard Labor to consist of Oakum Picking, Mat Making, or other Industrial Labor.

Time.	Class	Hard Labor, 1st Class.	Hard labor, 2nd class	Employment.	Promotions and Remissions.	Relaxations.	Restrictions.
1st week	1	8 hours Tread Wheel, Crank, or Stonebreaking, and 2 hours Oakum Picking.	10 hours Oakum Picking	10 hours Oakum Picking, 2 hours in the open air	1 good Mark required every day to raise to Class II.	Bible & Prayer Book, no secular book	Sleep on Plank Bed, no Mattress
Remainder of 1st month	2	8 hours Tread Wheel, Crank, or Stonebreaking, and 2 hours Oakum Picking.	10 hours Oakum Picking	10 hours Oakum Picking, 2 hours in the open air	1 good Mark required every day to raise to Class III.	Bible & Prayer Book, no secular book	Sleep on Plank Bed, no Mattress
2nd & 3rd month	3	8 hours Tread Wheel, Crank, or Stonebreaking, and 2 hours Oakum Picking.	10 hours Oakum Picking	2 hours Oakum Picking, and 8 hours Industrial Labor	55 good Marks required to raise to Class IV. Remission of 1 day in 10, to be reckoned in Class VI.	Slates and secular books, if convicted for first time. May write and receive one letter	Sleep on Plank Bed, no Mattress for 2nd month
4th, 5th & 6th month	4	6 hours Tread Wheel, Crank, or Stonebreaking, and 4 hours other labor.	6 hours Oakum Picking, and 4 hours other labor	10 hours Industrial Labor or other employment	80 good Marks required to raise to Class V. Remission 1 day in 7, to be reckoned in Class VI.	As above even if previously convicted	
7th to 12th month inclusive	5	4 hours Tread Wheel, Crank, or Stonebreaking, and 6 hours other labor.	4 hours Oakum Picking, and 6 hours other labor	10 hours Industrial Labor or other employment	156 good Marks required to raise to Class VI. Remission 1 day in 7, reckoned in Class VI.	Slates, &c. as above, and may write and receive one letter every 3 months. One hour's Exercise if at work in cells	Sleep on Plank Bed, no Mattress
Remainder of Sentence	6	2 hours Tread Wheel, Crank, or Stonebreaking, and 8 hours other labor.	2 hours Oakum Picking, and 8 hours other labor	10 hours Industrial Labor or other employment	Remission 1 day in 7. Each day gained in previous Classes to exempt from 2 hours Tread Wheel or Crank, to reckon at end of Sentence.	As above	As above

Prisoners to be in the same class in Dietary as in Labor Table. Promotion from Class to Class to be dependent on industry and good conduct. Prisoners may be degraded to a lower Class for misconduct, subject to the opinion of the Medical Officer before any reduction of Diet is made. The Medical Officer to determine the description of Hard Labor a Prisoner is competent to perform. Prisoners for Hard Labor for 14 days or less, to do 10 hours Oakum Picking, and not to leave their Cells except to go to Chapel. Female Prisoners sentenced to Hard Labor to pick not less than 3 lbs. of Oakum a day, unless their labor be required in the services of the Prison. Prisoners in Class 4, 5, and 6 may receive education out of hours appointed for other Labor.

Rules respecting Marks.

Industrious Prisoners whose conduct is good to receive one good Mark daily, thus—(1).
Prisoners careless or not sufficiently diligent to receive one indifferent Mark, thus—(0).
Idle or badly conducted Prisoners to receive one bad Mark, thus—(—).
N.B.—Indifferent Marks leave Prisoners Stationary. One bad Mark cancels one good one.
All Oakum issued to Prisoners will be weighed when picked. Prisoners may be allowed to see their respective Mark Register, and may appeal thereon to the Governor or Deputy Governor.

75. THE DIETARY FOR PRISONERS.

28, 29, Vic. c. 126, Sec. 21.

Meals	Days of the Week	Articles of Food	Class 1 (One week or less) Men	Women	Class 2 (After 1 Week and up to the 1st Month inclusive) Men	Women	Class 3 (After 1 Month and up to the 3rd Month inclusive) Men	Women	Class 4 (After 3 Months and up to the 6th Month inclusive) Men	Women	Class 5 (After 6 Months) Men	Women
			Ounces	Ounces	Ounces	Ounces	Ounces	Ounces	Ounces	Ounces	Ounces	Ounces
Breakfast	Every day	Bread	6	5	6	5	8	6	8	6	8	6
		Gruel	··	··	1 pint	1 pint	1 pint	1 pint	1 pint*	1 pint*	1 pint*	1 pint*
Supper	Every day	Bread	6	5	6	5	6	6	8	6	8	6
		Gruel	··	··	··	··	1 pint	1 pint	1 pint	1 pint	1 pint*	1 pint*
Dinner	Sunday	Bread	8	6	8	6	10	8	10	8	12	10
		Cheese	··	··	1	1	2	2	3	2	3	2
	Monday, Wednesday and Friday	Bread	6	5	6	5	4	4	4	4	4	4
		Potatoes	··	··	··	··	12	8	16	12	16	12
		Suet Pudding	··	··	··	··	8	8	12	8	12	8
		Indian-meal Pudding	6	4	8	6	8	6	8	6	8	8
	Tuesday, Thursday and Saturday	Bread	6	5	12	8	8	6	8	6	16	12
		Potatoes	8	6	··	··	8	8	8	6	12	8
		Soup	··	··	··	··	¾ pint	¾ pint	1 pint	1 pint	1 pint	1 pint

Ingredients of Soup.

In every pint:

The meat and liquor from 6 ounces of the necks, legs, and shins of beef, weighed with the bone, previous to cooking.

1 ounce of onions or leeks.

1 ounce of Scotch barley.

2 ounces of carrots, parsnips, turnips, or other cheap vegetable, with pepper and salt.

On Tuesdays and Saturdays, the meat liquor of the previous day is to be added.

Ingredients of Suet Pudding.

1½ ounces of suet.

6¼ ounces of flour, and about 8 ounces of water to make 1 pound.

Ingredients of Indian-meal Pudding.

To consist of half-a-pint of skimmed milk, to every 6 ounces of meal.

Ingredients of Gruel.

To every pint, 2 ounces of coarse Scotch oatmeal, with salt.

* The Gruel for breakfast on Sunday in Class 4, and for breakfast and supper in Class 5, to contain 1 ounce of molasses.

Male prisoners at Hard Labor, at Treadwheel, Crank, Flax and Rope Beating, and women employed in the laundry or other laborious occupation, to have the following additions and substitutions.

In Class 2.—1 ounce extra of cheese on Sundays, and one pint of gruel for supper daily.

In classes 2, 3, 4, and 5.—1 ounce extra of cheese on Sundays.

In lieu of the pudding on Mondays and Fridays—3 ounces of beef in class 3; 4 ounces in Class 4; and 4 ounces in Class 5 for men; and 2 ounces in Class 3; 3 ounces in Class 4; and 3 ounces in Class 5, for women.

The meat to be weighed after cooking, and served cold.

The meat liquor on Mondays and Fridays to form part of the soup on Tuesdays and Saturdays.

The soup to contain in each pint 2 ounces of split peas, instead of 1 ounce of barley.

for fraud, and deserters *en route*, the diet of Class 3.

Prisoners under punishment for Prison offences under the provisions of the 42nd Section of the Prison Act, to have the Diet of Class 1 for the first seven days; and after that to have 2 ounces extra of bread per diem.

Prisoners may be placed in a lower Class of the Dietary by order of a Visiting Justice, with the sanction of the Medical Officer.

H

Prisoners for examination, before trial, misdemeanants of the first division who do not maintain themselves, and destitute debtors, the diet of Class 3 without Hard Labor, for any period not exceeding one calendar month; that of Class 4, after the expiration of one month, and till the completion of the second calendar month; and that of Class 5 if the detention should exceed two calendar months.

Debtors or bankrupts committed by county courts, or by any court of law

Library

The precursors of the public library were the reading society's, the first established in 1766.

In Savage's 1822 edition of Toulmin's History of Taunton he describes the development of the early societies and how they operate:

In the same year that Savage brought out the History of Taunton, The Taunton and Somerset Institute was formed in the New Market. It had an extensive

'There are three reading rooms and two circulating libraries in Taunton. The oldest reading room is that of the market-house, which is supplied with four daily London newspapers, and four provincial weekly ones.

Savage's reading room and library, in the High Street, has upon the table four London daily newspapers, nine provincial weekly newspapers, and the Votes and Proceeding of the House of Commons, during the session of parliament.

Smyth's Reading Room and Library, in Fore Street, is supplied with three London daily papers, and seven provincial weekly papers.'

library and museum. It closed in 1883. The Somerset Archaeological and Natural History Society was formed in 1849 and established an extensive library and is still flourishing today.

The Public Libraries Act was introduced in 1850 by William Ewart with further amendments in 1853 and 1855. However, it required a local referendum in the borough and for ratepayers to vote in favour by a two-thirds majority for a public library to be instituted. On this basis it was rejected twice in Taunton in 1883 and 1888   before being adopted in 1902.

The library in Corporation Street was built in 1904 by Colburne. Little and Goodson from a red sandstone brick, with a grant of £5,000 from the trust set up by the millionaire philanthropist, Andrew Carnegie. It was extended in 1912.

The first annual report on lending from the library in Corporation Street showed 3,529 books in stock

The old Library, now the Pitcher and Piano, in Corporation Street.

in the lending department and 1,417 copies in stock in the reference department. This steadily increased over the years so that in 1934 there were 21,092 copies in stock, 37,000 in 1951, 70,000 in 1969 and now well in excess of that figure. Whereas 41,481 books were lent out in 1905, there were nearly 500,000 in 2007.

Another library opened in Priorswood in 1968. A local history library opened in the Castle in 1973.

A new library was begun on the site of a supermarket in Paul Street in March 1995 and opened in February 1996. It covers a total area of more than 3,000 feet square, incorporating two specialist local libraries: the Somerset Studies Library and the library of the Somerset Archaeological and Natural History Society. The last two specialist libraries are

The 'new' library in Paul Street

to be relocated to a new site off Silk Mills along with Somerset Record Office (presently in Obridge Road) in 2010.

Lighting
Oil lamps were first introduced in 1791, though they were not very effective.

In the spring of 1816, an engineer called John Ride of East Reach, Taunton, who specialised in water-driven engines, produced gas from a home-made plant. He was not the first in his field, preceded as he was by Frederick Windsor who had formed the Gas, Coke and Light Company of London in 1812. Together with the watchmaker and jeweller Thomas Lake, it is thought that he was principally responsible for setting up a gas lighting company, though within a year it had failed. A new venture, though, was planned in 1821, the Taunton Gas Light Company. The site eventually settled on was in Holway Lane (now South Street) where the Eagle Inn was later situated. It came into being in February 1823 with the purpose of 'lighting the town of Taunton and places adjacent with gas.' A gas maker named John Bailey was employed as well as a Lamplighter named John Creed. Both were given houses on the side of the site at Holway Lane.

It was erroneously thought that oil gas was a better option than coal gas. After experimenting with a number of alternatives including whale oil and linseed oil, it was decided to convert to coal gas in 1833. By 1834, a total of 44 gas street lamps were established in the town.

There was an exhibition of electric lights on the parade outside the Victoria Rooms as early as 13 January 1879. These were arc lamps that were powered by batteries. On the 20 January there was a floodlit football match between Taunton and Wellington near Wellington railway Station. This time the arc lights were powered by a generator.

In August 1884 Henry Massingham, owner of a boot and shoe company, used electric light for a musical fete at the site of the current County Ground (then the Taunton Athletics Club). He persuaded the borough council and the market trustees to allow a trial which took place from 1 May 1886 when seven arc lamps illuminated the town in the Parade, North Street, High Street and Fore Street.

A reproduction 1886 arc lamp in Goodland Gardens

They were powered by a portable engine driving a dynamo situated under the Eastern Arcade of the Market House. A seven year contract was agreed with Massingham. Taunton was the first town in the southwest to have permanent street lighting. Permanent plant was positioned in premises adjoining the 'Old Angel Hotel' opposite the Municipal Buildings (removed when Corporation Street was built). In 1890, the Taunton Electric Lighting Company built a power plant in St. James's Street. It was sufficient to run 120 arc lamps and 2,500 incandescent lamps. It ran from sunset to midnight only. However, the company was a financial failure and was bought out by Taunton Council in 1893 for about £10,000, thus passing the responsibility for lighting to the ratepayers. The overhead mains wire was put underground and a new boiler was purchased at a cost of £5,000. By 1910, arc lamps had been replaced by incandescent lights which required less maintenance.

A plaque erected on the side of the Market House in 1886 commemorating the 100th anniversary of street lighting in Taunton

Lisieux

Taunton's twin town since 1955.

Situated east of Caen in the Basse-Normandie region in the Calvados Department. It is the chief town of three cantons. The population of the town is 23,166 and of the metropolitan area as a whole is 45,065.

It was inhabited by the Gallic tribe Levixii. Today, inhabitants of Lisieux are known as Lexovviens, from this period. The Roman name was Noviomagus.

Commune of Lisieux

The first Bishop of which we are aware is Theodibandes from a reference in 538. A successor of his, Freculfus who died in 850, wrote a universal history. From the year 1000 to the French Revolution it was governed by the court of the bishops. The concordat of 1801 united the diocese of Lisieux with that of Bayeux. From 1854 the Bishop of Bayeux took the title Bishop of Bayeux and Lisieux.

In the twentieth century Lisieux became a major centre of the French textile industry, at its height producing up to 30% of the countries textiles.

It suffered during the second world war, losing many of its fine wooden houses though many timber-fronted houses, which are typical of the region, remain. More than 800 were killed. It was liberated by allied troops on 23 August 1944.

The most notable building is the Basilique de Saint Therese designed by Louis M. Cordonnier, consecrated in July 1954 and finished in 1975. Sainte de Therese of Alencon, who devoted her life to the Carmelite order in Lisieux was canonised in 1925 and has been one of the most popular spiritual figures of the twentieth century in France. After Lourdes, this is the most visited pilgrimage site in France.

Another notable building is the Cathedrale de Saint Pierre built between 1170 and the middle of the 13th century. The towers and buttresses are later additions.

Basilique de Sainte-Therese.
Photo: Yummiefruitbat

A notable event was the first helicopter liftoff by Paul Cornu in 1907.

The local drink is sparkling cider. The region also famous for Calvados (Apple Brandy), the liqueur, Benedictine, and the creamy cheese Pont l'Eveque, made at the town of that name to the north.

The twinning link between Taunton and Lisieux is one of the oldest twinning links in the country. A working party was set up in 1948 with Mr Reginald Trevett, a French leader at Huish's Grammar School and Wing Commander Winn, as joint secretaries. The two towns were considered compatible in that they were both market towns of a similar population with cider-making and dairy-farming important to the surrounding area.

After a visit by Mr Trevett to Lisieux in 1949 and a meeting with Monsieur Parmin who had taught at Newton Abbot Grammar School, and the friendship that ensued, a first official visit led by the Mayor of Taunton took place the following year leading to the establishment of the Taunton-Liseux committee and the civic link became firmly established. The visits between the towns arising from the link have been so successful that in 1966 the friends of Lisieux was formed as a purely social twinning link in which anyone from the Taunton area is invited to join the experience.

Lynch Law in Taunton

'We understand that several persons have had their handkerchiefs and purses stolen by some of the Swell Mob. We hear that Miss Luttrell had her purse stolen. One of these rascals was taken in the act of purloining a handkerchief, and lynch law was adopted. He was taken to a pump and thoroughly drenched, and then had his ear split so that he might be known again.' Sherborne Journal, 20 September 1849.

Market House, The

A Market House was built in the early 1680's by subscription. It had pillars and an assembly room on the first floor. However, by the middle of the 18th century it seems that a new building was required.

The former Market House in Taunton

A Market House Act came into being in 1768 for the construction of a market house in 'a spot of ground, so crowded with buildings, in the centre of town, besides obstructing the free circulation of air, could not be attended with many inconveniences and nuisances, by the filth lying in the passages, and the receptacles for idleness and vice, which many of its buildings, from their situation became.'

Not surprisingly, given the above, the erection of the Market House was preceded by the demolition of a number of buildings, including a number of public houses and the medieval Guild Hall. The specific purpose of the new Market house building was 'for preventing the holding of any market in the streets of the said town.' The act also resulted in the building of 'a large pavement of broad flag stone, two hundred and sixteen feet in length and eighteen feet in width, called the Parade.' The Market House was of red brick and two-and-a-half-storeys. It was completed in 1772 by Coplestone Warre Bamfylde of Hestercombe. It contained a Guild Hall, a Reading Room, Assembly Room, Card Room and Billiard Room.

Although there were moves to replace it with a new Town Hall in the late 19th century it remains in use as commercial and retail premises, albeit with the removal of the two arcades either side in 1930 (to enable road widening) and their replacement with two-storey attachments.

In 1821 the trustees were responsible for building the New Market House in Fore Street. It later changed its name to the Victoria Rooms and in 1934 to the Town Hall. It was taken down in the 1960's. The Corn Exchange was built in 1853 adjacent to Castle Bow. From 1910 to 1933 it was in use as a cinema. The building was demolished in 1937 to make way for the Electricity Board Showrooms (now Next).

Marshall, William

He visited the vale of Taunton in September 1794, describing it as 'The Golden Vale.' In his book, *The Rural Economy of the West of England*, in the section on 'Climature' in west Somersetshire he says, 'The climate, particularly of that part which is called *The Vale of Taunton Deane*, is particularly mild and serene; and the soil highly fertile and productive. The eye is agreeably relieved by a judicious mixture of arable and pasture; and if it be contrasted with some parts of the Northern District, it may emphatically be called the Land of Canaan.'

Mary Street Unitarian Chapel

The current chapel was built in 1721 or slightly later on the south side of Mary Street, though there was a Baptist Chapel in existence here it is thought as early as 1646.

It was built of brickwork, later rendered. The front was altered in the late 19th century to include two tiers of pilasters.

By the beginning of the 18th century the congregation come to accept Unitarian doctrines. John Wesley preached here on several occasions. Joshua Toulmin, the first historian of Taunton, was its Minister for 39 years from 1765. While living at Nether Stowey, Coleridge came to preach at the chapel. It still has the original interior and an 18th century candelabra.

Mayor, The

In 1627, Taunton became a corporation with a mayor. The first mayor was Andrew Henley. However, the right to a corporation was taken away with the Restoration in 1661.

A new charter was granted by the King in 1677, despite recent acts of rebellion against the crown in Taunton. They refused to pay taxes in 1662 and rioted against taxes in 1667. The manor rents were stolen from the Castle in 1664 (resulting in execution of the perpetrators) and in 1680, Thomas Dare personally handed in a petition from Taunton requesting Charles II not to allow the

Catholic James II to be considered for the succession. The eleventh of May celebrations celebrating the Royalist's withdrawal to Bridgwater during the Civil War in 1645 were vigorously supported each year, much to the displeasure of the King.

When Stephen Timewell was elected mayor in 1682 he attempted to bring Taunton back in line with the loyalist cause. He tried to quash the Eleventh of May celebrations of 1683, though he met with resistance. Lord Stawell reported to the Secretary of State, Sir Leon Jenkins, 'They (the crowd) were very rude with him.... and would have stoned him to death if he had not made an honourable retreat.' However, he was not deterred. Those who refused to take the Oath of Allegiance were likely to be sent to prison and, in the August following, he records

Myer Jacobs, the first mayor under the new charter of incorporation which was granted in 1877.

how 'We burnt ten cart loads of pulpits, doors, gates and seats upon the market place....the bells rang all night....the fanatics dare not open their mouths.' However, only two years later Taunton was to welcome the Duke of Monmouth and begin a further wave of rebellion.

The charter was lost again after a quarrel over the choice of a recorder in 1792. The final charter of incorporation was not granted until 1877 when Myer Jacobs was elected. It was he who had been the prime mover behind the establishment of the new charter. However, his fitness to serve was questioned with the following extraordinary letter printed in the Somerset County Herald of 14 July 1877.

'Sir, - it appears to be very generally supposed that you, who have become our Mayor are an unbaptized person and, consequently, not a Christian. If, as I hope is the case, there be no truth in this supposition, will you authorize me publicly to say so, and thus relieve many persons, in our town from an exceedingly painful and distressing impression I propose to publish this letter together with any answer you may send to me - I am,
Your obedient Servant, F. J. Smith, Vicar of St, John's Taunton.
To the Worshipful Mayor.

REPLY

Rev. Sir, - I have received a letter bearing your signature, and, but for recognising your writing, should have deemed it a forgery. I am proud to avow myself a member of the Hebrew faith. I am equally proud to know that my Christian neighbours and friends have not permitted religious differences to influence them in the choice of their first Mayor.
I shall not permit anything to mar the pleasure I feel in subscribing myself,
Myer Jacobs, Mayor of Taunton.

In 1974 with local government reorganisation the borough of Taunton became Taunton Deane Borough Council and it is to the Deane as a whole that the Mayor now owes his allegiance.

The Mayor is elected for one year from one of the 54 Deane Councillors. The mayor has a practical and a ceremonial role. In his or her practical role he or she leads the council and acts as chairman. The ceremonial role of the Mayor involves such tasks as welcoming important visitors to the town, heading major celebrations or events or visiting new businesses.

There are two important symbols of office. The first is the Mace, a symbol of authority, originating as a weapon. It has been adapted over the years to a symbolic role, sporting a crown and the coat of arms. The current mace was presented in 1877 by two members of parliament, Sir Henry James QC and Mr A. C. Barclay. The previous mace disappeared in about 1820.

The second symbol of office is the mayoral chain. The chain, with a medallion depicting a coat of arms was presented to the borough council in 1884 by Alderman Thomas Penny. Shields were added each year until the inauguration of Taunton Deane in 1974 (68 in total). The chain is 18ct gold and the overall weight is 750 grams. There is also a chain for the mayoress which is 14ct gold and has a medallion which shows the royal crown in diamonds. There are 37 shields attached containing the names of previous mayoress's. It weighs 190 grammes. It was presented by Mr T. S. Penny in 1928.

On special occasions the mayor wears a large red cloak with fur around the edge and a black hat with a heavy gold chain.

The Sergeant at Mace accompanies the Mayor at most ceremonies. He or she is responsible for the mace, chain and robes.

The Ornate top of the mace

Taunton: An A - Z

Members of Parliament from 1529

Two members were returned for the Taunton constutuency until the Redistribution of Seats Act of 1885 when one member was returned.

Date	MP Name	MP Name	Date	MP Name	MP Name
1529	Thomas Cromwell	Not Known	1754	George Carpenter	John Halliday
1539	Not Known	Not Known	1761	Robert Maxwell	George Carpenter
1542	Not Known	Not Known	1768	Alexander Popham	Nathaniel Webb
1545	Not Known	Not Known	1774	Nathaniel Webb	Edward Stratford
1547	Sir Nicholas Hare	John Caryll	1780	John Roberts	John Halliday
1553(Mar)	Not Known	Not Known	1790	Sir Benjamin Hammett	Alex. Popham
1553(Oct)	James Bassett	Jaques Wingfield	1796	Sir Benjamin Hammett	William Morland
1554(Apr)	William Barnes I	Oliver Vachell	1802	William Morland	John Hammett
1555	Thomas Eden	John Norris	1806	John Hammett	Alex. Baring
1558	Valentine Dale	Richard Myrfield	1807	John Hammett	Alex. Hammett
1562	Miles Sandy	Anthony Leigh	1812	Henry Powell Collins	Alex. Baring
1571	Robert Hill	Richard Blount	1818	Sir William Burroughs	Alex. Baring
1572	Robert Hill	Richard Blount	1820	John Ashley Ware	Alex. Waring
		(died 1575)	1826	Henry Saymour	William Peachey
		Edmund Hody	1830	E T Bainbridge	H Labouchere
1584	Alexander Pym	John Goldwell	1831	E T Bainbridge	H Labouchere
	(died 1585)		1832	E T Bainbridge	H Labouchere
	Maurice Horner		1835	E T Bainbridge	H Labouchere
1586	Francis Bacon	John Goldwell	1837	E T Bainbridge	H Labouchere
1588	John Goldwell	Thomas Fisher	1841	E T Bainbridge	H Labouchere
1593	William Aubrey	John Davidge	1842	T E Colebrooke	J Hall
1597	Edward Hext	Edward Barker	1847	Sir T E Colebridge	H Labouchere
1601	Daniel Dunne	John Bond	1852	H Labouchere	A Mills
1660	William Wyndham	Thomas Gorges	1853	Sir J W Ramsden	H Badcock
1661	Sir William Portman	Sir Wm. Wyndham	1857	H Labouchere	A Mills
1679	Sir William Portman	John Trenchard	1859	G A F C Bentinck	A C Barclay
1681	Edmund Prideux	John Trenchard	1865	Lord William Hay	A C Barclay
1685	Sir William Portman	John Sanford	1868	A C Barclay	H James
1689	Sir William Portman	John Stanford	1873	H James	Sir A F A Slack
1690	Sir William Portman	Edward Clarke	1880	Sir W Palliser	Sir H James
	(Died 1690)		1882	Viscount Kilcoursie	S C Allsop
	John Speke		1885	Samuel Allsop	
1695	Edward Clarke	John Speke	1887	Alfred Allsop	
1698	Henry Portman	Edward Clarke	1895	Alfred Chomeley	
1701(Jan)	Henry Portman	Edward Clarke	1906	Edward Boyle	
1701(Nov)	SIr Francis Ware	Edward Clarke	1909	William Wellesley Peel	
1702	Sir Francis Ware	Edward Clarke	1912	Sir Gilbert Alan Willis	
1705	Sir Frencis Ware	Edward Clarke	1918	Denis Fortescue Boles	
1708	Sir Francis Ware	Edward Clarke	1921	Sir Arthur Griffith-Boscawen	
1710	Sir Fracnis Ware	Edward Clarke	1922	John Hope Simpson	
1713	Sir Francis Ware	Edward Clarke	1924	Andre Hamilton Gault	
1715	Sir Francis Ware	Edward Clarke	1935	Lt-Col Edward Wickham	
1722	James Smith	John Trenchard	1945	Victor Collins	
		(died 1724)	1950	Henry Hopkinson	
		Abraham Elton	1956	Edward du Cann	
1727	Geroge Speke	Francis Fane	1987	David Nicholson	
1734	Francis Fane	William Berkeley	1997	Jackie Ballard	
1741	Sir John Chapman	John Buck	2001	Adrian Flook	
		(died 1724)	2005	Jeremy Brown	
		Percy O'Brien			
1747	Sir Charles Wyndham	Robert Webb			

see also **Potwallopers**

95

Merton, Guy of

The first prior of the Priory of Taunton. He was an Italian appointed by William Giffard, Bishop of Winchester in about 1125 He was felt to have too great a concern for the welfare of the poor and he was transferred to Bodmin!

Monmouth Rebellion

In 1685 Taunton became the centre of a rebellion against the new 'papist' King, James II.

James Scott, the Duke of Monmouth

James Scott, the Duke of Monmouth was the illegitimate son of Charles ll. His mother was Lucy Walters. His illegitimacy did not prevent him from being favoured by his father and he was appointed Commander in Chief of the British Army in 1672 and Captain-General in 1678. Military success in the third Anglo-Dutch war as well as his Protestantism made him popular with many English people though his popularity did not extend to the aristocracy and they did not like his association with the common man.

James Stuart, the Duke of York and Charles's brother revealed himself as a Catholic and was in line to replace Charles on the throne. This was anathema to many of the English people as they feared a repeat of the persecution of Protestants that took place under 'Bloody Mary'. This was particularly keenly felt in Taunton which had predominately sided with the protestant cause during the Civil War and had played an important role in preventing a Royalist victory. There was also a very strong non conformist element which rejected the trappings of both churches and had suffered much persecution as a result, typified by the 1664 Conventicle Act which outlawed dissenting worship. On the accession of James after Charles's death in February 1685, Monmouth, residing in Holland, decided to act.

He set sail for the south west of England which he had toured five years before and where he had established his popularity. He had been promised a large army and hoped that he would be able to march into London unopposed. Landing at Lyme Regis on 11 June 1685 with only 82 supporters he marched north towards Somerset hoping thereby to garner support and swell his army. He marched first to Axminster where he gathered about 2,000 men. He failed, as he had hoped, to enlist the Duke of Albemarle to his cause with his militia of about 4,000 men who were in the area at that time. He gathered troops, who, though they were no doubt determined and committed to their task, lacked military training and equipment as their weapons were old or substituted with farm implements. This is why it is sometimes known as the Pitchfork Rebellion. The anticipated support from London and East Anglia was also not forthcoming.

Monmouth and his men marched into Taunton on 18 June 1685. Before his arrival rumours of a rebellion abounded and likely rebels had been locked up. However, the militia under Lord Stawell had panicked and left town. Here he was welcomed. The town was festooned with flowers and 115 year old Elizabeth Broadmead 'Walked in procession' before him. He stayed the night at Captain John Hucker's house opposite the Three Cups Inn.

The next day, some of the townsmen forcibly freed the prisoners. There was a procession of 26 young women led by one Sarah Blake carrying an unsheathed sword and a bible. On receiving these gifts he said 'he now came into the field, with a design to defend the truths contained therein, and to seal it with his blood, if there should be an occasion for it.' However, unfortunately, he had not managed to find support among any of the important families which would have been critical to his success. The next day in Taunton on Saturday 20 June he was proclaimed King. Three proclamations were made. James ll was declared a usurper and £500 was put on his head, the English parliament was declared to be a seditious assembly and the Duke of Albermarle, who was within a few miles of Taunton, was declared a traitor. His ranks had swollen to six thousand but the delay in Taunton may have been critical.

From Taunton he went to Bridgwater where he was also welcomed. His declaration was read and voluntary contributions were raised. He travelled on to Glastonbury and Wells where again he was proclaimed King. From Wells he continued to Shepton Mallet where an attack was planned on Bristol via Keynsham.

However, on advancing to Bristol the weather turned bad and Monmouth decided to return to Keynsham where they lost 20 men to the Royalist forces. Because the Royalist forces appeared to be so close and the fact that Beaufort commanded 4,000 men in Bristol, Monmouth decided not to attack Bristol after all. This was probably an error as he was looked upon favourably there and with the resources of the town at his disposal he might well have been

The beheading of the Duke of Monmouth at Tower Hill on 15 July 1685.

able to mount a successful attack on the capital.

Instead they advanced on Bath. This was, though, a Royalist town with a strong garrison. He changed his mind again and turned towards Frome. On his way he was greeted by the demoralising news of the Duke of Argyle's defeat at Inchinnan. Argyle's plan had been to stir rebellion in Scotland but he was captured at Inchinnan on 19 June and executed on the 28 June. Monmouth also heard of the King's advance from London. He proceeded at last to Bridgwater via Shepton Mallet and Wells where he had heard that there would be 10,000 men ready to fight at his side. However, when they entered the town on the 3 July there were only 160. Monmouth at first thought that he might strengthen his position at Bridgwater but the advancement of the King's troops under the Earl of Faversham and Lord Churchill resulted in their encampment in Sedgemoor around Westonzoyland and Chedzoy.

At about 2 in the morning on the 6 July he attempted a surprise attack on the King's troops across the marshy wastes of Sedgemoor. However, the rebel troops were spotted, the element of surprise was lost and, in the darkness, they had difficulty finding the ford which led to the Royalist Camp. Monmouth's cavalry soon retreated. The infantry proved an easy target for the Royal Cavalry. As it became light the Royalists under the Earl of Faversham launched a joint cavalry and infantry attack and Monmouth's army was routed. It is thought that the Royalists lost about 80 men to more than a 1,000 on the Duke of Monmouth's side. On the 9 July Colonel Kirke entered Taunton with prisoners and wounded and in the afternoon hung 19 of them outside the White Hart Inn.

Monmouth had fled and had been discovered in a ditch disguised as a shepherd. He was taken prisoner and transported to London. There was no need for a trial as he had already been condemned by an act of parliament. He was brought to Tower Hill where he was beheaded on the 15 July.

Judge Jeffries

The Bloody Assizes. Between the 17 and 19 September Judge Jeffreys held his Bloody Assizes in the Great Hall of Taunton Castle. He dealt with 526 cases. 19 were hung in Taunton and a further 139 were sent to be hung in neighbouring towns and their remains deliberately displayed around the county for all to see the folly of rebelling against the King. 284 were transported. The young women who had approached the Duke of Monmouth were sent as a present to the Queens Maid of Honour. Some of them were later ransomed. Mary Blake who made the colours presented to Monmouth was committed to Dorchester Gaol where she died of smallpox, which was then rife in the prison. There seem to have been many who were condemned on the most spurious of evidence. Judge Jeffrey's reward when he returned to London was to be made Lord Chancellor (at 40). The horrors of those times lingered long in the memory of the people of Taunton.

Municipal Building

The Municipal Building began life as a boys grammar school in 1522 at the instigation of Bishop Fox, Bishop of Winchester and Lord of the Manor of Taunton Deane.

It took up to 160 pupils, predominately the sons of local merchants. During the siege of

The Old Muncipal Building, site of the first school

Taunton (1644-1645), the building was badly damaged by Colonel Blake and his men in battle against the King's forces. The school had to close but the building was reopened after building works and there were pupils for most of the time at the Hall until 1885 (though representing more than one school). Two years later, Taunton's corporation took over the building.

The building was added to and altered in the Tudor style in 1904, the newer part to the west of the main doorway.

It was listed as an ancient monument and a grade II listed building in 1933.

It became the home of the District Council after it was inaugurated in June 1973 and remained so until 1987 when the Deane House opened in Belvedere Road. It is now used as a Registry Office, by the Mayor and a variety of voluntary bodies for meetings. It is a grade II listed building.

Newspapers

The first printing press in Taunton was in 1716 and was owned by William Norris who produced the first edition of the Taunton Journal on Friday 21 May 1725.

The cost was one-and-a-half-pence which included a halfpenny stamp. It was printed in large type.

Stamp duty came into being in 1712 at a halfpenny a copy. It was said to be a means of raising revenue though, in fact, there is no doubt that it was intended to restrict the activity of the press and, in particular, its availability to the working classes. In 1797 it was raised to three-and-a-half pence and by 1815, it had reached four pence a copy. There was also an advertisement tax of one shilling per advert which was introduced in 1812 rising in stages to as much as 3s and 6d per advert. This was crucial as adverts were the papers main source of revenue. It was reduced to 1s 6d in 1833 and abolished in 1853. Stamp duty was abolished in 1855.

After the abolition of stamp duty the number of newspapers produced greatly increased. While it is tempting to make a direct connection with the abolition of the duty, other developments at this time also have to be taken into account. Improvements in the quality of road surfaces and the coming of the railways aided distribution while improvements in the education system meant more people could read. This was allied to improvements in printing technology.

There were two attempts to make the Somerset County Gazette, which is still printed, into a daily newspaper. In the first instance, between January and June 1878, it ran as the Somerset County Daily Gazette and in the second instance, between June 1882 and September 1884, as the Daily Somerset County Gazette.

There was very little of local interest in the early papers. They mainly consisted of national news or reports from abroad. However, at the end of the nineteenth century as relatively inexpensive national daily papers became established, local newspapers began to concentrate on local issues.

An early edition of the Taunton Journal

Taunton Newspapers (Produced in Taunton)

Start Date	Name	Finish Date (where known)
21 May 1725	Taunton Journal	
8 May 1742	Somerset, Bath & Somersetshire Journal	
2 Mar 1793	Taunton Herald & Weekly Advertiser	23 June 1797
22 Sep 1808	Taunton & Courier Western Advertiser	1 July 1936
30 Mar 1811	Taunton & Bridgwater Journal	
31 Dec 1836	Somerset County Gazette	present
17 Jan 1845	Somerset County Herald	
18 June 1855	Illustrated Western News	22 Oct 1875
July 1855	Western News	10 May 1920
1 May 1857	Taunton Gazette & Farmer's Journal	
1859	Western News & Farmers' Market Reporter	
1 Sep 1860	Taunton Chronicle	24 Nov 1860
1 Dec 1860	Clarke's Taunton & Somerset Chronicle	31 May 1862
7 June 1862	Somerset Chronicle	
1865	Taunton Farmer's Journal	
?1865	West Somerset Chronicle	
12 Jan 1866	Western Herald	25 Oct 1867
1 Nov 1867	Western County Herald	1 May 1868
6 June 1868	Taunton Weekly Advertiser	28 Aug 1868
16 May 1868	Webb's Advertising News	1875
?1870	Taunton Patriot	
1873	Devon & Somerset Weekly News	
10 Jan 1874	Somerset County Chronicle	
17 Apr 1875	Taunton Sun	28 Oct 1876
18 Sep 1875	Taunton Gazette & Western News	25 Dec 1875
1876	Western Observer	
Jan 1878	Somerset County Daily Gazette	22 June 1878
5 June 1882	Daily Somerset County Gazette	27 Sep 1892
5 Mar 1887	Somerset Express	10 June 1878
9 Mar 1887	Taunton Echo	10 June 1933
28 Oct 1889	Western Farmer & Gardener's Chronicle	28 Feb 1892
18 April 1894	Taunton Mail	9 May 1923
1934	Somerset County Advertiser	
1998	Taunton Times	2006

Produced in Taunton covering other areas

Start Date	Name	Finish Date
12 Jan 1866	Axbridge & Cheddar Gazette	28 Nov 1867
22 Sep 1885	Yeovil & Chard Chronicle	27 Apr 1892
1896	Minehead Mercury	28 Dec 1899
1896	Wiveliscombe Express	28 Dec 1928
6 Jan 1896	Milverton Mail	28 Dec 1899

The Taunton, Wellington & Wiveliscombe Flying Post was printed in Yeovil. Nine editions were produced in 1866.

Newton, Vicar George

He went to Exeter College Oxford. His first ministry was at St Peter and St Paul, Bishop's Hull. He was instituted in St Mary's Taunton in 1631. Of strong Puritan conviction he was influential in the group that sailed to America in 1636 to help found Taunton, Massachusetts. With the outbreak of the Civil War in 1642 he went to St Albans to escape the attentions of the Royalists who initially held Taunton. On his return in 1655 with the climate favourable he invited Joseph Alleine to be his assistant. After the restoration of Charles ll, he and Alleine, who both felt they were unable to accept the Act of Uniformity which required them to use the latest book of Common Prayer, were ejected from the church. They continued to preach though it was Alleine who was by far the most active and openly flouted the rules. He was imprisoned twice and suffered ill health resulting in his death at the age of 34. After the Act of Indulgence in 1672, Newton became licensed as a Presbyterian preacher and became the first minister of Paul's Meeting.

North Street Congregational Church

It was established on the former site of Whitmash's Wagon Yard after 65 members of the Paul's Meeting congregation broke away to form their own church in June 1843. The site was purchased for a £1,000 and the new church built for £1,500 by Samuel Pollard.

The Rev Henry Quick was invited to preach the first four sermons and then invited to move his ministry from London to the Taunton church. A school and a vestry were added in 1845 and in 1850 galleries, to accommodate an increasing congregation. An organ was installed in 1870. It was from this congregation that the initiative came for the establishment of the West of England Dissenters' Proprietary School (later Taunton School). Along with Paul's Meeting and Silver Street Baptist Church money was raised to establish Rowbarton Congregational Church near St Andrew's Church in 1910. It was demolished in 1971. A new organ made by the Taunton firm of Osmond's was installed in North Street Church in 1939.

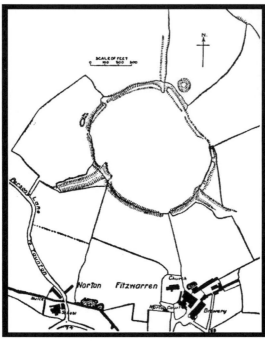

Earthworks at Norton Camp

Norton Hill fort

A large circular Bronze Age Hill Fort just outside Taunton.

About 3 miles from the centre of Taunton the hill fort was an important settlement long before the growth of Taunton. The saying goes, 'When Taunton was a furzy down Norton was a market town'.

The fort lies at the top of a low hill about 50 metres high and consists of large circular earthworks about 250 metres in diameter, surrounded by a bank and a ditch and covering about five acres in total. Access to the central site is possible from three entrances. The ditch lies inside the hillside enclosure which suggests that it was not originally used for defence. Tom Mayberry speculates, 'It may have been used as a ceremonial site or as a trading centre on the frontier lands between tribal areas lying east to west.'

There is a theory that 4,000 years ago a large henge monument may have existed to the north of the fort. There is definite evidence of occupation from about 3,500 BC from bronze-age pottery found on the site. Eight bronze bracelets and two kinds of axe were found during an excavation in 1908 by Harold St George Gray. It was during the Iron Age the site was developed into a hill fort surrounded by a ditch. Though Roman pottery as well as Bronze Age and Iron Age artefacts were found in the 1908 excavation, it is not thought likely that there was a Roman settlement here. If there was a Roman settlement in this area it is more likely to have been at Monty's Court in the village of Norton Fitzwarren.

Further excavations by Nancy and Philip Langmaid between 1968 and

1971 led to the discovery of mesolithic and neolithic flints, as well as Bronze Age bracelets, axe-heads and other metalwork. A neolithic axe-head was discovered in 1981.

Later tradition had it that a fearsome dragon inhabited the hill fort as depicted on the chancel screen in Norton Church.

Norton Hill Fort

Northgate

First mentioned in 1158. It stood at the south end of Tone Bridge near to the turning for St James Street.

Noxious Effluvia

Edward Goldsworthy describes in his 'Recollections' written in 1883 how, in his youth, 'in the autumn months (when the drains were choked for want of rain, and the water was low in the river)' there was the presence of 'diarrhoea, dysentery, fevers and other diseases.'

In 1821, James Lackington Rice of his own volition put sewers into the centre of Taunton. Though they were an improvement on the open drains that preceded them they were of poor design, discharging directly into the Tone. It was not until the Board of Health was established in 1849 (opposed by the Market Trustees) that the situation seriously improved. In 1872 an Urban Sanitary Authority was formed and in 1877 a sewage works was opened at Lambrook. Various processes were experimented with including the Sodium Process, Aluminoferric, Lime and Coppers. However, none of these processes was capable of giving sufficient purification to allow the effluent to be admitted to the river. This was not achieved until the introduction of a system of septic tanks at the beginning of the twentieth century. In 1919 the average daily 'sewage' flow was 850,000 gallons. By the mid 1950's it had reached nearly 2.5 million gallons. A new works was begun in April 1954 by consulting engineers A.H.S. Waters and Partners and was opened on 20 June 1957 by the Mayor, Councillor R. F. Winckworth.

Pageant, Historical 1928
(See Defendamus)

Like Biscuits Oughta Be!

Palmer, George 1818 -1897

Apprenticed to Mr Hitchcock, the Taunton baker and confectioner, he then moved to Reading to join Thomas Huntley whose father, Joseph, had founded a biscuit and bakers confectionary in 72 London Street but had been forced to retire through ill-health. Thomas did not have his father's good sense and it was George who brought the enterprise and skill to the biscuit-making process. He quickly doubled the size of the bakery and introduced machinery. They moved to larger premises in King's Road in 1846. By 1860, Huntley-Palmer was the largest biscuit maker in the country.

Penny's

The Penny's left a considerable mark on the town in the Rowbarton area of Taunton. Thomas Penny (1827-1906) moved from Leicester and worked for timber merchant George Pollard of Taunton before setting up in business for himself in 1885. He bought the Greenway Estate and, together with his son, also Thomas, built many of the houses that make up the western part of Rowbarton. If you have ever wondered at the names in this part of Taunton you have to look no further than Thomas Penny's sons and grandsons. Thus, Cyril, Leslie, Raymond, Herbert, Thomas and William all gave their names to streets. Many of the other names originate from liberal statesmen (Roseberry, Asquith, Gladstone and Harcourt) and the Baptist preacher Dr John Clifford (Clifford Avenue).

Population

Population comparisons are complicated by the shifting nature of boundaries. Toulmin's population survey of 1790 was made by visiting individual houses but was more accurate than anything went before. In his survey he confined himself to the parishes of Bishop's Hull and Wilton inside the turnpike gates 'or to the contiguity of houses, except where the borough reaches beyond the gate leading to Pitminster.'

Until the census of 1861 the figures that were available were for St Mary's and St James's parishes, though they did not cover some parts of the town and extended beyond it. I have used these figures until 1891, even though figures for the slightly more populous parliamentary borough were available in 1831 and from 1861 - 1881, as it makes for easier comparison. From then on I have used the figures for the Municipal Borough (created in 1885), though this is also shifting ground as there were extensions to the borough boundaries in 1921, 1932, 1958 and 1966 before its abolition in 1974. The population for the first census after this in 1981 is based on the electoral wards for Castle & Wilton, Fairwater, Galmington, Halcon, Holway, Lyngford and Rowbarton. There are some further changes to the electoral wards included for the 1991 and 2001 census though they are roughly equivalent. There was no population census in 1941 because of the war.

1086	1,500	1901	21,087
1790	5,300	1911	22,561
1811	6,997	1921	23,223
1821	8,534	1931	25,179
1831	11,139	1951	33,620
1841	12,066	1961	35,192
1851	13,119	1971	37,444
1861	13,720	1981	35,482
1871	14,368	1991	42,148
1881	15,620	2001	53,290
1891	18,026	2008	60,400 (estimate)

Post Office

In 1822 the post office was in North Street opposite the Castle Inn, about 80 metres from the present office. In the 1822 Savage's edition of Toulmin's History of Taunton we are told:
'The mail from London, by way of Bath, Wells, Glastonbury, and Bridgwater, arrives in Taunton about three o'clock in the afternoon and proceeds, through Wellington and Cullompton, to Exeter. It returns in the morning at half-past nine, and sets off from Taunton to London, at ten o'clock. Letters

Post Office in North Street

for London and all places eastward of Taunton, should be in the office before eight in the morning: and for Exeter and all places westward of Taunton, by two in the afternoon. The postmistress is Miss Sarah Daw.'

It then moved to Hammett Street where it remained until the new post office was opened in North Street in 1911 at the site of the Spread Eagle Inn. In this time a sorting office was established at the railway station and following the Post Office Parcels Act of 1882 the Post Office started handling parcels which had previously been the preserve of the railways.

Potwallopers

Tom Locke, the last of the Potwallopers Picture by Harry Frier SANHS

Before the passing of the Reform Bill in 1852 in some areas there were Potwalloper Boroughs. Taunton was such a borough. A potwalloper was strictly someone who had a hearth on which to boil a pot. In effect, this gave the vote to many Taunton males though it precluded paupers or those receiving charitable relief, and of course, women. Though this type of franchise was abolished by the Reform Act of 1832, the existing potwallopers were allowed to vote. The last known potwalloper in Taunton was Tom Locke who died aged 94 in 1904. An alternative name was potwalloners, as described by Defoe in his 'Tour of the Island of Great Britain'.

Though it might seem that Potwalloper Boroughs were more democratic than other types of boroughs where ownership of land, say, was the qualification for voting, they were open to a great deal of abuse. There was no secret ballot until 1872. Goldsworthy says: 'The elections in Taunton were a disgrace to all England.' Bribery and corruption were the order of the day. Beer and tickets for beer were given to women and children as well as men. 'The first candidate's arrival was made known by several hogsheads of beer being rolled in the Parade. It was then drawn off in buckets, pitchers and jugs and most of it consumed on the spot; the effect of which was soon both audible and visible, by singing, shouting, swearing and fighting amongst the men, and screaming, cap-tearing and hair-pulling by the women.'

Toulmin in his History of Taunton provides many examples of corruption at election time. The example of the 1774 election was a good case in point. The election result was challenged. Nathanial Webb and Edward Stratford were returned on a poll of 260 votes and 240 votes as against that of John Halliday and Alexander Popham, who polled 202 and 201 votes respectively. The 'losing' candidates and several electors, however, lodged an appeal which was upheld. A committee found:

'That the mayor had rejected many legal votes, which were tended for the petitioners, and admitted many illegal votes for the sitting members:
'That the petitioners were duly elected, by a great majority of legal votes, and ought to have been returned:
'That the sitting members previous to, and during, the election, were guilty of bribery and corruption, by themselves and agents.'

Potwalloper boroughs were abolished with the 1832 Reform Act though the franchise was not greatly extended until the Reform Acts of 1867 and 1884. The secret ballot was not brought in until 1872 under the government of William Gladstone.

Priory

Taunton Priory was founded as an Augustan house in about 1120 by William Giffard, Bishop of Winchester. Henry de Blois provided the land for a new Priory close to the present site of St James's Church in about 1158.
The Priory land extended from the boundary ditch in the

Site of Taunton Priory as depicted in a late 19th century drawing

west to St Margaret's Leper Hospital in the East and from the River Tone in the North and East Reach in the South. It also owned land known as Priors Wood on the further bank of the Tone and land and churches in several of the villages beyond. In 1162 it is recorded that eleven churches and chapels, including the main church of St Mary Magdalene, belonged to the Priory.

Unfortunately, little remains of the Priory following its destruction in 1540 as part of the Dissolution of the Monasteries. There is a building known as 'The Priory Barn' dating from about the late 15th century. It was probably accommodation for guests or lay members. The Priory Church was dedicated to St Peter and St Paul and contained the chapels of St Anthony, St Theodric and the Virgin Mary. The order dressed in black robes. There were 26 canons in 1339, twelve when the deed of surrender was signed in 1539.

The Canons, as in all walks of life, it seems were a mixed bunch. The scholarship of Guy of Merton, the first prior of the Priory of Taunton, was highly thought of and he was devoted to the welfare of the poor. In fact, he was felt to have too great a concern for the welfare of the poor and he was transferred to Bodmin, which it seems at that time was akin to being transferred to Siberia. In 1345 Canon de Payton is pardoned for the rape of the wife of Hugh de Holden and of stealing from him. In 1353, Canon Robert Cunyat was gaoled for living an immoral life and disobeying and threatening his prior.

Taunton Priory survived for more than 400 years. It was at the centre of religious life during the middle ages. The buildings were ransacked and destroyed as part of the Dissolution of the Monasteries in AD 1540.

During 2004 an archaeological excavation took place at the former County Garage adjacent to the junction of Priory Avenue and Gyffarde Street, carried out by Context One Archaeological Services. It had been known that Priory lands included a lay cemetery, the only one for the population in and around Taunton. St Mary's, for example, did not acquire the right to bury its own dead until 1446. The excavation showed that the site included part of the cemetery with the discovery of the remains of bodies (adding further to an earlier excavation at Canon Street). The other significant find was a good part of the site of the Priory Church itself where a wall two metres thick and foundation pads two metres square were revealed. One estimate puts the church at 60 metres long and 20 metres wide. Three stone-lined tombs were also found, two of which contained the bodies of adult males. Two other adult males were found in the vicinity of the central tomb.

Provost of Penhryn

One of the hated tax collectors of a tax imposed in early 1497 to finance an English campaign against the Scots. Several thousand marched from Cornwall towards London in protest. The provost of Penrhyn fled from Cornwall but was captured by some Cornish rebels near Taunton. He was brought into the market place in Taunton and dismembered and cut into pieces. The march into London ended in defeat at Blackheath on 17 June of that year.

Quaker Meeting House

The first reference to the Quakers, or members of the Religious Society of Friends, in Taunton is in 1654 when John Cam and John Audland visited from the north of England to 'spread the word'.

The first Taunton Quaker who we are aware of is Elizabeth Calway by virtue of the fact that she was brought before the justices for being rude about one of the vicar's in Taunton -

The Quaker Meeting House in Bath Place

suggesting he was deluded. Quakers were often persecuted and would meet within each others houses or in the open, in fields or in orchards.

As they grew in number the need for a meeting house became clear and in 1693 Robert Button left a house and some adjacent land in present day Bath Place, then known as Hunt's Court. The grandson of Robert Button, Joseph Jefford, left over a £1,000 to the Society of Friends in 1801. In 1813 it was decided at a meeting the friends to seek an estimate for a new building. It was paid for from the money left by Jefford (though some wrangling over the Will meant the full amount was not forthcoming), and in part by subscription. In addition, Anne Rison gave some small plots of land to the Friends in lieu of an annual obligation to maintain the iron railings. A cottage was erected next to the meeting house in 1831, now the Caretaker's Cottage. A verandah was removed about 20 years ago and a lavatory and a small kitchen have been added by means of a small extension. Though the meeting house was originally designed to take a large gathering, the meetings throughout the twentieth century have generally been small. There was particularly poor attendance after the First World War when sometimes no meetings at all were held. There were several occasions when it was suggested that the meeting house should be closed down and sold. However, in recent years, gatherings have substantially increased.

Quaker Tapestry. The Quaker Tapestry is a modern embroidery of 77 panels made by 4,000 men, women and children as part of an international community project exploring three centuries of social history. It was conceived at a Taunton meeting. It has been exhibited at the Exhibition Centre in Kendal, Cumbria, the traditional northern homeland of Quakerism.

Queen's College

Queen's College was founded following a meeting in November 1842 in the vestry of the Temple Chapel in Taunton. The aim was 'a respectable school on moderate terms and on strictly Wesleyan principles.'

The Wesleyan Proprietary Grammar School, as it was then called, was first established as a girl's school at a temporary site in rooms within the Castle grounds that had previously been occupied by a ladies seminary at an annual rent of £40. Taking the title Castle House, it took its first pupils in July 1843. The fees were between 21 and 27 guineas for borders and 9 to 11 guineas for day pupils, depending on age. The headmistress was a Mrs Symonds. By 1865 it had outgrown the premises and moved to Mount House. Castle House became a private boys school and in 1843 became a Weselyan school.

The number of pupils soon increased to over 100 and in October 1844 it was decided to look for a site to build a school. Six acres were purchased on Trull Road for £1,200 and a tender was accepted by a Mr John Mason of Exeter. The architect was the noted James Wilson of Bath. Knapp stone was supplied from a quarry in North Curry. The cornerstone was laid by Rev John Scott in April 1846 and it was opened the following year. It now took on the shortened name of the Wesleyan Collegiate Institution.

The first headmaster was Thomas Sibly who appeared to be well ahead of his time. As Channon states in his comprehensive history of the school, 'In the days of "Dotherboys Hall" and the "Hungry Forties" Sibly believed the schoolboy should be well fed, and was opposed to corporal punishment.'

In other respects the regime appeared to be quite harsh. For example, it was stated that no conversation was allowed in the day rooms, in the dormitories or to and from the Temple Church, a considerable walk from the school.

In its early years the school struggled. Pupil numbers began to decline and in 1852 £2,700 was borrowed in order to pay the bank. In May 1855 Sibly handed in his resignation. However, the directors had complete confidence in him. His salary was raised to £400 a year with a bonus if the pupil numbers reached a particular level. He withdrew his resignation and stayed for another 27 years.

Difficult years followed the end of Thomas Sibly's reign. The overdraft at the bank increased and numbers dropped though academic success remained at a similarly high level. However, the school was stabilised under the headship of A. S. Haslam who was the head from 1899 to 1926.

The school was renamed Queen's College in 1887.

Racing, from Taunton

There were races at Broomhay, Taunton from 1788 but these were abandoned after 1812. Racing moved to Bridgwater beside the River Parrett and then returned to Taunton in 1825 at the site of the present King's College in South Road. It is estimated that crowds were as much as eight or nine thousand strong.

In 1838 heavy rain washed out the course and in 1840 the races were moved to Trull Moor. Here they stayed until 1855. Racing continued after this date at Bridgwater but ceased at the beginning of the First World War. It was not until 1927 that racing returned to Taunton when, on 25 July seven men met at the Paddington Hotel in London to found the Taunton Racecourse Company. The location for the course was the site of Orchard Portman House which had been demolished in 1840. The first meeting, the Shoreditch Sell-

ing Hurdle, took place on 21 September and was won by Mr Rayson's Baalbek.

When the M5 Motorway was built, some of the waste soil was used to build up and extend the bends and the back straight. The clay soil has also been drained to improve racing conditions throughout the year.

There are approximately 14 race meetings a year of the National Hunt from November and April. It is the youngest Jump Racecourse in Britain.

On 18 April 2008 Grand National Winner Comply or Die ridden by Timmy Murphy was paraded at the Taunton Racecourse. He was trained by David Pipe of the nearby Pond House Stables at Nicholashayne near Wellington. He is the son of legendary trainer Martin Pipe who retired in May 2006 after nearly 20 years when he dominated National Hunt Racing. (He trained Minnehoma to a Grand National Win in 1994 and won the Champions Hurdle in 1993 and 1997 with Granville Again and Make A Stand, while also enjoying considerable success on the Flat). This was a dream start for David Pipe , in only his second season as a trainer.

Railway

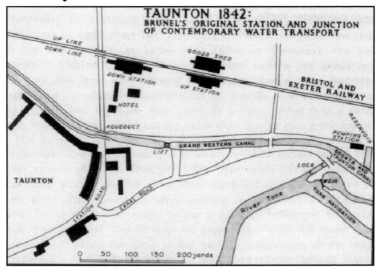

Plan of Taunton Station, 1842

In July 1842 Brunel's Bristol and Exeter Railway reached Taunton. The Taunton Courier describes how 'much excitement prevailed, the line now connecting the town with Bristol, Bath and London.' The engines were 'richly decorated with various banners.' In celebration about a hundred sat down 'to an elegant spread at the Station Hotel.' Brunel was cheered when he joined the assembly later on.

The West Somerset Railway from Taunton to Watchet was completed in 1862. In 1874 it was extended to Minehead. The line was converted to narrow gauge in 1882. The line was closed in 1971 (though it later reopened as a private steam railway).

In 1866 a Taunton to Chard line via Ilminster was opened. This spelt the end for the recently cut Taunton to Chard Canal. It was converted from broad gauge to narrow gauge in 1891.

In 1871 the Devon and Somerset Railway was opened from Norton Fitzwarren to Wiveliscombe. Two years later it reached Barnstaple. The route was difficult and involved lots of tunnels and railway cuttings. It was converted from broad gauge to narrow gauge in 1881. It was taken over by the Great Western Railway in 1901 and closed in 1966.

Whilst the railways meant the end of the canals as far as commercial traffic was concerned, they also benefited from the infrastructure of the canals in that steam engines required a large volume of water each day. Creech Pumping Station, in particular, played a vital role in providing water for the thirsty engines on the Paddington to Penzance route. Two new steam engines were installed to replace the existing beam engine in 1901 to supply the engines that required over 100,000 gallons of water a day.

Railway Accidents

There were two railway accidents at the same time of year in Norton Fitzwarren though seperated by almost 50 years.

The first was on 11 November 1890, A special mail train from Plymouth, bound for Paddington, crashed into a stationery goods train in Norton Station. The signalman had forgotten that the goods train was still on the main line and cleared the approach of the mail train. At 1:24 am the mail train ran into the goods train at an estimated speed of 50 m.p.h. The driver and fireman managed to jump clear but did not have time to issue any kind of warning. Eleven passengers were killed and eight injured. The enquiry into the incident came to the conclusion that there were contributory factors. The guard of the goods train was required by company rules to notify the signalman that he was on the main line. This was not done in this case. Also, the goods train headlamp was changed from red to green when it still should have shown red. This may have not have prevented the accident completely, but may have triggered the application of the brakes by the driver of the mail train.

The second incident occurred on 4 November 1940. The train, the King George VI, set off from London on time at 9.50 pm bound for Penzance, via Bristol. It remained on time until, due to an air raid, the train lost time somewhere around Bristol. This must have been troubling for the engine driver, Percy Stacey, as he and his family had been made homeless only a few days previously when his house in Acton had been bombed. The train arrived in Taunton 68 minutes late at 3.30 am. It was stormy and dark and a gale was blowing. The driver was diverted to the relief line rather than the main line which this train normally

The wreckage of King Geroge VI and carriages which crashed on 4 November 1940 at Norton Fitzwarren

travelled on. He did not realise he was on the relief line and read the signals for the main line, which were green. When he saw a mail train passing him he realised he was on the relief line, shut off the steam and applied the brakes. The train left the rails. The engine was plunged onto its side and the first three railway carriages telescoped.

This was only fourteen months into the war. Many passengers mistook the crash of the train for a bomb.

The locomotive, the King George VI, was later repaired and returned to service.

Other railway accidents include a derailment at Creech in 1852 which caused the death of an engine driver and the stoker and on 30 April 1907 when the 9 am train from Chard collided with a goods train at Obridge Junction about 500 yards from Taunton Station. Though three of the carriages were torn apart by the force of the impact only seven of the sixteen passengers were injured and the two drivers were both unharmed.

In the post steam era, on 6 July 1978, eleven people died and seventeen were injured when fire broke out on the Penzance to Paddington sleeper train half-a-mile outside Taunton. Used bed linen had been stacked in a plastic bag against an electric heater in a British Railways Mark 1 Coach number W2437 built in 1960. A serious fire broke out. Unfortunately, the ventilation system of the train drew air from the coach which meant, as the fire developed harmful carbon monoxide gases were being inhaled by the passengers. By the time the train was stopped at 2.41 near the Silk Mills signal box just outside Taunton after a communication cord had been pulled, a number of passengers were already dead. The rescue of passengers was hampered by the fact that some of the train doors were locked in contravention of the rules at the time. Injured passengers were taken to Musgrove Hospital.

The fire had far-reaching consequences for the design of the new mark 3 coaches where the specifications were upgraded to include higher grade fire retardant materials and alarm systems, as well as revised emergency procedures.

Richard of Taunton Deane

The following ballad, also known as Dumble Deary Dum, was printed on various broadsides (a printed sheet of lyrics of popular songs). One in the Bodleian Library is dated 1837.

Last New Year's Day, As I've heard say,
Young Richard he mounted his dapple grey,
And trotted along to Taunton Deane,
To court the parson's daughter Jean.
Dumble-dum, dumble-dum deary,
Dumble-dum, dumble-dum, dumble-dum dee.

With buckskin breeches, shoes and hose,
Dicky put on his Sunday clothes,
Likewise a hat upon top of his head,
All bedaubed with ribbons red.
Dumble-dum, dumble-dum deary,
Dumble-dum, dumble-dum, dumble-dum dee.

Young Richard he rode without any fear,
Till he came to the house where lived his sweet dear;
When he knocked and he kicked and he bellowed 'Halo!
Be the folks at home? Say aye or no!'
Dumble-dum, dumble-dum deary,
Dumble-dum, dumble-dum, dumble-dum dee.

A trusty servant let him in,
That he his courtship might begin;
Young Richard he walked along the great hall,
And loud for Mistress Jean did call.
Dumble-dum, dumble-dum deary,
Dumble-dum, dumble-dum, dumble-dum dee.

Miss Jean she came without delay,
To hear what Richard had got to say.
'I s'pose you know me, Mistress Jean,
I'm honest Richard of Taunton Deane.'
Dumble-dum, dumble-dum deary,
Dumble-dum, dumble-dum, dumble-dum dee.

'I'm an honest fellow, although I be poor,
And I never were in love afore;
My mother she bid me come here to woo,
For I can fancy none but you.'
Dumble-dum, dumble-dum deary,
Dumble-dum, dumble-dum, dumble-dum dee.

'Suppose that I were to be your bride,
Pray, how would you for me provide?
For I can neither sew or spin,
Pray, what will your day's work bring in?'
Dumble-dum, dumble-dum deary,
Dumble-dum, dumble-dum, dumble-dum dee.

'Why, I can plough and I can row,
And zometimes to the market I go
With gaffer Johnson's straw or hay,
And yarn my nine pence every day.'
Dumble-dum, dumble-dum deary,
Dumble-dum, dumble-dum, dumble-dum dee.

'Nine pence a day! Twill Never do,
For I must have silks and satins too!
Nine pence a day won't buy us meat!'
'Adzooks! says Dick, 'I've a sack of wheat!'
Dumble-dum, dumble-dum deary,
Dumble-dum, dumble-dum, dumble-dum dee.

'Beside; I have a house hard by,
'tis all my own when mammy do die:
If thee and I were married now,
I's feed thee as fat as my feyther's old zow.'
Dumble-dum, dumble-dum deary,
Dumble-dum, dumble-dum, dumble-dum dee.

Dick's compliments did so delight,
They made the family laugh outright.
Young Richard took huf, and no more would say,
But he mounted old Dobbin and gallop'd away,
Singing *Dumble-dum, dumble-dum deary,*
Dumble-dum, dumble-dum, dumble-dum dee.

Rough Justice

In 1715 a Dragoon who stole a cheese escaped by jumping into the River Tone. His body was discovered several weeks later with the cheese still under his arm.

Royal Visits

Robin Bush wrote in his Book of Taunton, written in 1977, 'Only once since 1685 had the sovereign visited the town: in December 1937 when George VI passed swiftly through it.' However, on 20 June 1922, the future  King George VI did visit as the Duke of York in his capacity as the Colonel-in-Chief of the Somerset Light Infantry to meet his brother, the future Edward VIII who had been on a tour abroad. He met the Mayor and received a guard of honour on the terrace of the Municipal Buildings from the 5th Battalion of the Somerset Light Infantry before lunch at the Jellalabad Barracks.

The Queen did eventually visit, on 8 May 1987 and on 2 May 2002 in her Jubilee year. She is shown above visiting the Taunton Cider Factory on her 1987 visit. On her jubilee visit she visited the individual stalls of the Farmer's Market and then continued to Vivary Park where she was welcomed by thousands of school children. She also spoke to Doreen Hardman who had nursed her father George VI when he had lung cancer. She then visited the Red Cross Office and accepted a book on first aid.

Saint Andrew's Church

The impetus for the building of the church was the growth in population of that area following the arrival of the Great Western Railway. In fact, it became dubbed 'The Railway Parish' The original site was Chip Lane Fields but it was felt to be too close to St James's and not central enough for the congregation.

The land that was settled on was part of the orchard at Rowbarton House owned by a Mr Chubb. The architect was J. Houghton Spence and the builder was H. J. Spiller. It cost £2,500, paid for by the Rev Jeremiah Smith, the influential first vicar of Holy Trinity Church. The church is next to the school built by Rev Smith. Until the church was consecrated on the 14 July

St Andrew's Church

1881 services were held there.

The church was enlarged and re-dedicated in 1893 due to an increase in the congregation by Spiller at a cost of £5,000. The original south aisle was removed and a new larger south aisle added. A Lady Chapel was added and the High Altar was enlarged. This enabled 200 or so more to be seated in the church.

St George's Catholic Church

Originally based in the Crescent at the site of the current Masonic Hall (built in 1822.) Anti-Catholic legislation meant that a church with a tower could not be built. However, this changed with the Roman Catholic Relief Act of 1829. In response to a burgeoning congregation, land for the church at the  current site in Billet Street was donated by the Franciscan nuns based at the Convent in South Road. The church, with tower, was opened in 1860.

In 1959 the congregation had increased further so that another church was built at Eastwick Road, St Teresa of Lisieux, named after Taunton's twin town situated in northern France.

Saint James's Church

Thought to have been established in the 12th century. Like St Mary's, a large church. The font dates from the 15th

century and the pulpit from 1633. The tower is 120 feet high, rebuilt between 1871 and 1875. The stone came from quarries at Samford Brett donated by Sir Alexander Acland Hood. It is red sandstone in contrast to the limestone of the original tower. A new chancel was built between 1884 and 1885.

When the church tower was rebuilt they endeavoured to make it a facsimile of the first one. The biggest individual contributions were £500 from Mr Gore-Langton MP and £100 from Sir Alexander Acland Hood. Goldsworthy also describes in his book how £793 5s 5d was contributed from a bazaar. The total cost was £4,000

5s 5d. It is said that the tower rocks with the weight and force of the heavy bells as they are rung.

On top of the 120 foot tower there is a weather vane. The inscription on the Cock's wings are as follows:

A native am I and my name is Tom,
A jolly, gay bird, but I have no song,
I watch the wind, I keep events,
Which always have been my intents.

Saint John the Evangelist

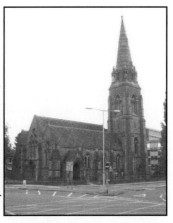

Dedicated in 1863. It was designed by Sir George Gilbert Scott. Highlights include a wrought iron chancel-screen and numerous stained glass windows.

The church was founded by the Rev F. J. Smith, who left Trinity Church to become its first vicar. It served at the time what was considered to be a poor part of Taunton.

Saint Mary's Church

Probably built as a result of the reorganisation of Taunton by Henry Blois, Bishop of Winchester, by about 1180. It is recorded that Richard Le Hose was killed when he fell from a beam in about 1240.

Its first incumbent was Simon de Lyme, appointed in 1308. During the 14th century it became known as the mother church.

The roof dates from Tudor times. The porch, originally built in 1508 was restored by the incumbent vicar, Dr Cottle , in 1805. The tower was originally built in the late 15th /early 16th century. By the middle of the 19th century it had become unsafe. It was rebuilt over four years and completed in 1862 by Benjamin Ferrey and George Gilbert Scott with Wilton stone provided by Sir Alexander Hood. The arcade between the two north aisles dates from 1508.

Simon Jenkins in his book 'The Thousand Best Churches' describes the tower as 'the finest in all England. It makes peace with the sky not just with a coronet but with the entire crown jewels cast in red-brown sandstone.'

The oldest bell dates back to 1616 (recast in 1885). In 1633 it was recorded that the bell tower would sway when all the six bells were rung. The heaviest bell is the tenor which weighs 30 cwt and was cast in 1861. Over the years the number of bells has been increased to twelve.

Donkey on The Edge
One of the most arduous jobs during the rebuilding of the west church tower was the hauling of stones by pulley as the tower was built. The responsibility was with a donkey. When the tower was near its completion he would walk nearly the length of Hammet Street in order that the stone could be raised to the top. His reward on the completion of his work was to be hoisted to the top of the tower to admire the fruits of his own labour. Afterwards, he was looked after and put out to a grass.

Sewell, Joseph

The blind giant who died in Taunton in 1829.

He originally came from Lincolnshire and lodged with a carpenter in Church Square of the surname Luxton. According to Goldsworthy, 'a kind-hearted tradesman (Mr John Bluett) cared for him and paid his funeral expenses.'

Siege of Taunton

The 'Siege of Taunton', in which Blake and his Parliamentarian troops resisted Royalists attempt to take the town, was remembered in song and later through an opera and as part of a pageant (see seperate entry under Defendamus)

The castle was occupied by parliamentary troops on 5 June 1643. The Royalists took control until June of the following year when Laurence Chislet of St James's parish who had been held prisoner in Taunton for 20 weeks escaped and brought news to the parliamentary generals at Lyme Regis that the garrison at Taunton at that time only consisted of 80 men (when formerly it had consisted of 800). Robert Blake of Bridgwater marched with 500 men from Lyme Regis and succeeded in forcing the Royalists to surrender on the 5 June 1644 after a week of siege.

Lord Hopton, the Royalist Commander who retreated to Bridgwater on the 11 May

Having taken the town Blake put up earthworks to defend his position at the main East Gate into the town, at the East Gate of the Castle and also near Saint Mary Magdalene. The Royalists laid siege to the town in October with 3,000 men under Colonel Edmund Wyndham. Repeated cannon fire from the north across the river caused considerable damage and a breach was made in the castle wall. It is also thought likely that the roof of the great hall was brought down at this time. Blake's men were driven back into the castle. A parliamentarian relief force from Chichester drove the Royalists away.

Fearing another attack, Blake extended a ring of earthworks in the new year. At the beginning of April the attack on the town was renewed by the Royalists under Lord Goring with 6,000 men at his disposal. The town had been encircled and the water supply cut off. At the beginning of May, the Royalists with their ranks now swollen to eight thousand made a determined onslaught. East Reach and East Street were taken and the town was fired. When asked to surrender Blake gave his celebrated reply that he would eat three of his four boots before he surrendered. A parliamentary relief force arrived in Taunton on the 11 May to find the Royalists under Lord Hopton had already retreated to Bridgwater believing that the whole army under Fairfax was on its way when, in fact, it was a brigade under Colonel Ralph Weldon, the rest of the army having been sent to Oxfordshire.

This was not quite the end, for Lord Goring made a further attempt to capture Taunton in June. However, he gave up on the 3 July. A week later he was defeated at the Battle of Langport.

Siege - the Song

The retreat of Hopton to Bridgwater was long celebrated in acts of public devotion and anniversary sermons and by the following song:

The Eleventh of May

The Eleventh of May was a joyful day,
When Taunton got relief;
Which turned our sorry onto joy,
And eased us of our grief.

The Taunton men were valiant then
In keeping of the Town,
While many of those who were our foes
Lay gasping on the ground.

When Colonel Massey, of the same,
Did understand aright,
He, like a man of courage bold,
Prepared himself to fight.

With that our soldiers one and all
Cast up their caps and cried,
What need we fear what man can do,
Since God is on our side?

Taunton: An A - Z

Long time did Goring lie encamped
Against fair Taunton Town;
He made a vow to starve us out,
And batter our castle down.

Within our castle did remain
(A garrison so strong)
Those likely lads which did unto
Poor parliament belong.

Before daylight appeared in view,
The news to them was come
That goring and his cursed crew
Were all dispersed and gone

But who can tell what joy was there,
And what content of mind
Was out into the hearts of those
Who's been so long confined?

Our bread was fourteen pence per pound,
And all things sold full dear;
Which made our soldiers make short meals,
And pinch themselves full near.

Our beer was eighteen pence per quart
(As for a truth was told),
And butter eighteen pence per pound
To Christians there was sold.

The Cavaliers dispersed with fear,
And forced were to run,
On the eleventh of May, by break of day,
Ere rising of the sun.

Let Taunton men be mindful then
In keeping of this day;
We'll give God praise with joy always,
Upon th'eleventh of May.

Siege of Taunton - the Opera

On the 14 April 1898 an opera was staged at the London Hotel Assembly Rooms (later the County Hotel) and was based on the events surrounding the Siege of Taunton during the Civil War, though the details of the story were entirely fictional.

It had been written the year before by the Somerset cricketing all-rounder, George Nichols. The music was composed by Harold Jeboult, the church organist at St Mary Magdalene Church with additional help by the organist Arthur Clements F. J. Moore. The town band's conductor, orchestrated the score.

The full title was *In the Days of the Siege - A Romance of Taunton.* Agnes Francis, the daughter of the Mayor, was in love with the Roundhead Ralph Snow. In order to save his life, after

> ## IN THE DAYS OF THE SIEGE.
>
> ~~~~~~~~
>
> #### ACT I.
>
> SCENE I.—*Exterior of the White Hart Inn.*
>
> ──────
>
> #### OPENING CHORUS.
> *Music by* HAROLD A. JEBOULT.
>
> GIRLS.   Though strictly guarded and confined
>   Within this ancient borough,
>   We leave our troubles all behind,
>   No grief shall leave its furrow.
>   So merrily we dance and sing,
>   And cast away all fears;
>   For maidens ne'er may care or fret,
>   Whose captors are gay Cavaliers.
>
> SOLDIERS.   Gay Cavaliers, bold Cavaliers.
>   Yes, cast aside your fears;
>   For though we're foremost in the fight
>   For Charles the good, the great, the right,
>   We for your beauty have an eye,
>   And fain would seek a sweet reply.
>   Yes, cast aside your thoughts of fears.
>
> GIRLS.   Gay Cavaliers, bold Cavaliers.
>
> SOLDIERS.   Gay Cavaliers, bold Cavaliers.
>
> MARGARET (*solo*).   List, gallant men, pride of our nation,
>   To a humble girl of low station;
>   Though I may appear unsophisticated,
>   Handsome Cavaliers are never underrated.

he was captured as a spy in a Taunton under Royalist control, she agreed to marry the Royalist Captain Freemantle. However, the marriage is not genuine, performed as it is by a friend disguised as a priest rather than a genuine priest. Snow escapes and returns with the Roundhead army under the leadership of Captain Robert Blake. The Mayor finally agrees to his marriage to Agnes and the production ends with a real wedding.

The local professional painter Harry Friar painted the scenery for the two scenes set at the White Hart Inn (The Parade) and the Castle grounds.

The opera was a resounding success with all three performances playing to a packed house. The profits were split between the Somerset County Cricket Club and the Taunton Town Band, which no doubt encouraged local support.

The local papers were enthusiastic, some of the national newspapers less so. A national tour, though, was arranged for the summer employing a professional cast. It opened at Weymouth and progressed to Plymouth, Taunton, Cardiff and Newcastle. Though it was generally well thought of, it did not transfer to London and money was lost on the tour. In 1900, however, the opera was revived as a means of supporting the reservist from Taunton who had gone to fight in the Boer War. The cast remained largely the same and with a few cuts and some minor additions and a new scene painted once again by Harry Friar. Between 18-20 January they once more played to packed houses at the London Hotel Assembly Rooms. Following the performance it was decided to form the Taunton Amateur Operatic Society.

Silk Making

Until the late 18th century fine thrown silk or organzine had been exclusively made in Italy. However, Sir Thomas Lombe spent time in Italy observing the manufacturing process and brought the secret back to this country, patenting a machine in Derby that was capable of producing silk of the same quality. In 1781 Vansommer and Paul of Pall Mall, London, purchased a brew house and premises from a Mr Noble of Upper High Street Taunton and installed a machine capable of producing quality silk. At the same time they entered into an agreement with a Mr Pounsberry, who occupied the adjacent bakery, to supply water. In 1783 the owner of a mill in Sherborne, Wilmot together with John Norman of Taunton bought the premises off Vansommer and Paul. In 1788, weaving was begun by Forbes and Wasdale. Crepe manufacture followed in 1795 introduced by Leney Smith of London. Further expansion in silk looms followed so that at the time of Publication of his History of Taunton in 1791 Joshua Toulmin could report, 'The number of looms employed amounts to about eight hundred in Taunton, and two hundred in the vicinity. There are about one thousand persons engaged in weaving, one hundred as winders and two hundred quillers. The throwing mills employ about five hundred persons; making the whole, about one thousand eight hundred persons'. By 1826 there were about 4,000 people depending on the silk industry for their work. However, with a reduction in the duty on foreign silk in 1829 a great influx of foreign raw silks followed so that silk making in Taunton soon began to decline. It did not completely die, though, and continued on a reduced scale. Pearsall's in particular, has continued to manufacture silk thread and now specialises in the manufacture of silk (and polyester) sutures from its premises in Taunton.

The Silk Mills from where the Silk Mills Road takes its name (Roughmoor) were formerly cloth works. They were destroyed by fire in 1833.

Silk Mills Bridge

The announcement that £10.6 million would be made available for a bridge to replace the Silk Mills railway crossing was made on the 15 December 2000.

This was part of the local transport plan which also included a Park and Ride scheme adjacent to the bridge for which there was

considerable opposition from the Bishop's Hull village residents.

The bridge was lowered into position on 2 April 2005, following three hours manoeuvring by a 1,200 tonne crane. This manoeuvre was the result of three years of planning between the construction company and the railway.

Over 800 bronze age artefacts were discovered during building work at the site of the bridge.

Skittles

There is a reference to the keeping of an illegal bowling alley as early as 1598 when Christopher Saunders and Thomas Garlick were prosecuted for keeping illegal bowling alleys. Presumably, gambling was involved. Skittles has long been a popular pastime in  Taunton and the surrounding area though many alleys have now been closed in order to offer space for dining areas. There is also competition from the Ten Pin Bowling alley at Hankridge Farm. However, many skittle alleys remain with a skittle league still going strong.

Smith, Reverend Sydney (1771-1845)

A preacher and lecturer he was seen as a radical at the time though now would be considered ahead of his time. He believed in the education of women, the abolition of slavery and the introduction of practical subjects into education. He was particularly vigorous in promoting Catholic emancipation.

In 1828 he was presented with a prebend in Bristol Cathedral which enabled him to keep a living at Combe Florey near Taunton simultaneously with that of Halberton attached to his prebend.

In 1831 he delivered his famous 'Mrs Partington Speech' in favour of the Reform Bill passed in 1832 in the Castle Hall in Taunton. He made a comparison between the House of Lords, who had just thrown out the Reform Bill, with Mrs Partington of Sidmouth, trying to stem the Atlantic Ocean with a mop:

'In the midst of this sublime and terrible storm, Dame Partington, who lived upon the beach, was seen at the door of her house with mop and patterns, trundling her mop, squeezing out the sea-water, and vigorously pushing away the Atlantic Ocean. The Atlantic was roused; Mrs Partington's spirit was up. But I need not tell you that the contest was unequal; the Atlantic Ocean beat Mrs. Partington.'

Somerset College of Art & Technology (SCAT)

Somerset College of Art and Technology can trace its origins to the School of Art in Bath Place (established in 1866) and the Technical Institute, which began in rented premises in the Upper High Street in 1891. The School of Art in Bath Place did in fact supersede a Mechanic's Institute that had been in Bath Place from 1840 to 1866 (Moving there from its original home in Paul Street). The School of Art remained in Bath Place until 1889 when it moved to the Victoria Rooms in Fore Street and then to a purpose-built building in Corporation Street in 1907. Meanwhile, the Technical Institute moved to Corporation Street (in the building that is now the Castle Moat Chambers pub) in February 1900. The institute included electrical, chemical and physical laboratories as well as classrooms and a lecture room. In 1950 it moved to the site of the former Bishop Fox's school in Staplegrove Road.

A new site was developed on Wellington Road in 1959 heralding the beginning of a new integrated site. The site in Staplegrove remained in use until recently when the main site was refurbished and expanded. It has now been sold off for housing.

Somerset Cricket Club

Formed in August 1875 after a cricket match between the Gentlemen of Somerset and a Devon side played at Sidmouth. The Somerset side were the winners.

They did not have a permanent home ground to begin with, using a variety of Somerset grounds for their home matches. It was not until 1882 they acquired a permanent home venue at the ground of the Taunton Athletics Sports Club which had opened the previous year beside the River Tone at its present site. In their first year one of their opponents were the Australians. They acquired first class status in 1891.

From a Photo by J. Chaffin & Sons, Taunton. Copyright.   London Stereoscopic Co., Photomezzotype.

A. E. Newton.	T. Spencer.	J. B. Challen.	W. N. Roe.	V. T. Hill.	T. Knigh
	(Hon. Sec.)				*(Scorer.)*
H. E. Murray-Anderdon.	S. M. J. Woods.	H. T. Hewett.	L. C. H. Palairet.	Tyler.	Nicho
(Hon. Sec.)		*(Capt.)*			
C. J. Robinson.		Capt. W. C. Hedley,		G. Fowler.	

SOMERSET, 1892.

The Somerset County Cricket Club Team in 1892

Though Somerset have never won the County Championship, they have won limited over competitions and league titles.

Their most successful year in terms of silverware was in 1979 when they beat Northamptonshire in the Gillette Cup by 45 runs and won the John Player League (now the Natwest Pro40 League). This was the beginning of the 'glory years' during which Ian Botham and Viv Richards starred. They were Benson and Hedges Champions in 1981 and 1982. There was a long period of fallow until they returned to their winning ways in the 2001 season when they won the

Cheltenham and Gloucester Trophy. Since then, in 2005. they have won the Twenty20 Cup (in only its third year) against Lancashire. In that same year they came second in the first division of the County Championship only to be relegated the following year. However, in the 2007 season they achieved promotion to the first division of both the County Championship and the Pro40 League.

First Class Record

Overall First Class Record

Out of a total of 2559 first class matches Somerset have won 604, lost 1010 and drawn 941. Four matches were tied and twelve abandoned.

Highest Team Total

Against Middlesex at the County Ground in Taunton between 18-21 April 2007.
Middlesex 600-4 declared
O A Shah (Owais) 193
Somerset: 850-7 declared.
Middlesex 209-2
Match drawn
J L (Justin) Langer 315

There are a couple of unusual things about this match, apart from the vast amount of runs scored. Firstly, the timing. Record breaking scores typically take place in the middle of a hot dry summer. This was the very first match of the season. However, this was a remarkably warm and dry April (followed by a remarkably wet summer).

Secondly, Middlesex batted first and had scored 600-4. When they declared they must have believed they were in a strong position. In total there were eight centuries shared between the two sides, a championship record.

Eight out of the ten highest first class scores by Somerset have been made since 2000.

Lowest Team Score

This was against old rivals Gloucestershire at the Ashley Down Ground, Bristol on 2 and 4 August, 1947. In their second innings (batting second) they could only scrape together 25 runs. There were six scores of nought. Without the 17 made by wicket keeper, F. S. Lee (Frank), things could have been much worse!

Somerset exacted an even more humiliating defeat against Gloucester at Fry's ground in Bristol in 1920. Batting second in their first innings Gloucester could only scrape together 22 runs. In the match as a whole, though, Gloucestershire had the last laugh. They won the match by 4 wickets.

Highest Aggregate Score (The total for both teams in all innings)

This was the match played between Somerset and Surrey at the County Ground between 3-6 July 2002. Surrey batting first scored 608 and 324. Somerset scored 554 and 329. The total aggregate score was 1815. The match was drawn.

Taunton: An A - Z

Tied Matches
There have only been 4 tied first class matches. Two of them were at the County Ground Taunton, against Sussex in 1919 and West Indies A in 2002. The third was against Essex in 1926 at the County Ground, Chelmsford. The last was at Chester Road North Ground at Kidderminster against Worcestershire in 1939.

Highest Individual Score
This was by Justin Langer in a match played between Somerset and Surrey at Woodbridge Road, Guildford. Opening the batting he hit 342 runs in 416 balls in 618 minutes. He hit 43 fours and 2 sixes. The Somerset total was at 688, their third highest team total on record. Though Langer made the highest individual score, Surrey, remarkably, outdid Somerset's total, scoring 717 runs.

Jamie Cox holds the record for the most runs in a match, narrowly ahead of Langer's effort of a few years later in a single innings. In 1999 against Hampshire at the County Ground in Southampton he scored 216 and 129 not out to make an aggregate score of 345.

Highest Partnership
The highest partnership was for the first wicket between L C. H. Palairet (Lionel) and H. T. (Herbert) Hewett against Yorkshire at the County Ground in 1892 when they made 346 together.

Most Runs in a Season
2761 By W. E. (Bill) Alley in 1961
Alley was an Australian who did not join Somerset until he was 38. He played his last game when he was 49. He then umpired first-class games for 16 years including ten test matches and nine one day internationals. He so loved the west country he stayed here rather than return to his native Australia when he retired.

Most Hundreds and Fifties in a Season
S. J. (Stephen) Cook scored 11 centuries in 1991. He also holds the record for the most fifties in a season when he scored 20 in 1990.

Most Ducks in a Season
B. (Bryan) Lobb had 16 in 1955.

Most Ducks for Somerset
93 by B. A. (Brian) Langford who played between 1953 and 1974.

The legendary all-rounder Sammy Woods (1867-1931) in the 1880's. Born in Sidney, he came to England when he was 14.
He played for Somerset between 1886 and 1910, captain 1894-1906. One of the few players to have played for England and Australia. He also played Rugby Union for England and Bridgwater and Albion.

Most Runs, Centuries and Fifties for Somerset
All three records are held by H (Harold) Gimblett who scored 21,142 runs and hit
49 centuries and 159 fifties.

Most Wickets in an Innings
Two bowlers have taken 10 wickets in an innings:
E. J. (Edwin) Tyler took 10-49 against Surrey at the County Ground, Taunton in
1895 and J. C. (John) White took 10-76 against Worcester at the County Ground,
New Road, Worcester in 1921.

Most Wickets in a Match
John White took 16-83 at the Recreation
Ground, Bath against Worcester in 1919.

Hat-Tricks for Somerset
There have been 17 hat-tricks for Somerset in total. The first was in 1882 by W.
H. (William) Fowler against Marylebone
Cricket Club at Lords, the last (at the time
of writing) by S.R.G. (Simon) Francis
against Loughborough University Centre
of Cricketing Excellence at the County
Ground in 2003. Only one man has taken
two hat-tricks and that was E. (Ernest)
Robson against Hampshire at the Recreation Ground, Bath in 1898 and against
Yorkshire at the County Ground, Taunton
in 1902. One M. E. (Marcus) Trescothick
took a hat-trick against Young Australia at
the County Ground, Taunton, in 1995.

Marcus Trescothick, Somerset and England

**Most Wickets and Five or More Wickets
in a Season**
A.W. (Arthur) Wellard holds both records for the same season. In 1938 he took
169 wickets and five or more wickets 17 times.

**Most Wickets for Somerset and Most Five Wicket Hauls in a Career for
Somerset**
These are both held by John White who took 2165 wickets and five or more wick-
ets 185 times.

Most Balls Without Conceding a Run
In the home match against Gloucestershire in the 1949 season, Horace Hazell
bowled 105 consecutive balls without conceding a run. He finished on 8-27.

Taunton: An A - Z

1,000 Runs and 100 Wickets in a Season
This has been achieved 8 times shared between five players. Top of the pile with 1,064 runs and 150 wickets in the 1929 season is J. C. (John) White. He also holds second spot which he achieved the following year with figures of 1,008 and 115 respectively.

5,000 Runs and 300 Wickets in a Career
This has been achieved by 18 players, including in the modern era I.T. (Ian) Botham and V. J. (Vic) Marks

Most Catches in an Innings
Five players have taken five catches in an innings. They were: J. (John) Daniel versus Kent at the County Ground in 1901, L. C. (Leonard) Braund versus Worcestershire at the County Ground in 1909, G. E. (George) Hunt versus Hampshire at Clarence Ground (Weston-Super-Mare) in 1928, P.J. (Peter) Robinson versus Lancashire at Clarence Park in 1968 and M. E. (Marcus) Trescothick against Gloucestershire at the County Ground (Bristol) in 2007.

Ian Blackwell, Somerset and England

Most Catches in a Match
This record is held by C. J. (Chris) Tavare with seven against Sussex at the Taunton County Ground. Five players have taken six catches in an innings.

Most Catches in a Career
J. C. (John) White holds the record with 393 catches in his time at Somerset.

Most Victims by a Wicket Keeper in an Innings
R. J. (Rob) Turner holds the record with seven victims against Northamptonshire at the County Ground in 2001. He also has been responsible for six wickets falling on four seperate occasions.

Most Victims by a Wicket Keeper in a Match
There have been five occasions when there have nine victims in a match. The first was by A. E. (Arthur) Newton against Middlesex at Lords in 1901. On the second occasion it was by H. W. (Harold) Stephenson against Yorkshire at the County Ground in 1963. The last three occasions have all been R. J. (Rob) Turner, against Yorkshire at Scarborough in 1996, Surrey at Taunton in 2001 and Derbyshire at Taunton in 2003.

Most Catches/Stumpings in a Season/Career

Harold Stephenson holds all these records. In the 1962 season he took 75 catches and in the 1949 season he made 44 stumpings. In total he took 694 catches in his career and made 312 stumpings.

Most Appearances

Brian Langford appeared no less than 504 times for Somerset between 1953 and 1974.

Mandy

Before his death on 28 December 2006 aged 92, Norman Mitchell-Innes was England's oldest surviving test cricketer. There is no longer an England test player alive who played in a test before the second world war.

Born in Calcutta of a Scottish family in 1914, he made his debut for Somerset at 16, while still at school at Sedbergh - where he once made 302 runs in a home match. He was in the middle of a boy's golf championship in Scotland at the time he was summoned. At Oxford university between 1934 and 1937 he scored a record-breaking 3319 runs.

Norman Mitchell-Inness

He particularly impressed by scoring 168 against the touring South Africa side in 1935 and was subsequently selected by Plum Warner for the England side at Trent Bridge. He only scored five but was kept on for the next test at Lords. However, he withdrew citing a bad dose of hayfever. He is quoted as saying, 'I might be sneezing just as a catch came in the slips'. He did suffer from chronic hayfever all his life. However, ironically, replaced by Errol Holmes who he was staying with for the weekend of the match, he did feel he was well enough to play for Oxford University against Surrey and, notwithstanding his hayfever, scored 132 not out. Errol Holmes meanwhile failed with the bat. Mandy, as he was universally known, was not selected for England again.

He had a good season with Somerset in 1936 but then joined the Sudan Political Service in 1937. He only played for Somerset while on leave and only 24 times after the war, unable to capture his pre-war form.

He played 132 first class matches and scored 6,944 runs. He hit 13 centuries and averaged 31.42. He took 82 wickets at 34.79.

He outlived his wife, Patricia Rossiter, whom he married in 1944. They had a son and a daughter together.

Taunton: the Home of Women's Cricket.

In August 2006 it was announced that Taunton was to become the permanent headquarters of women's cricket. Key matches and major domestic tournaments were to be held at Taunton with at least one women's international each year. In addition there were to be regional training camps throughout the year and improvements in the ground facilities. This is a joint initiative between the English Cricket Board and Somerset County Cricket Club, the first of its kind. In her interview with Somerset Sound, the England captain, Charlotte Edwards said: 'We're really excited about our new home and Taunton is a lovely ground and one we've always enjoyed playing at. The people in Taunton are so welcoming, too.

Somerset Light Infantry

The Light Infantry had its origins in the period during which the Duke of Monmouth threatened the throne.

In 1685 King James II asked the Earl of Huntingdon, Theophillus, to raise a regiment. It was known as the Earl of Huntingdon's Regiment of Foot.

When William of Orange came to the throne in 1688 the regiment transferred its allegiance and the Catholic Earl of Huntingdon gave way to the Protestant Ferdinand Hastings. The regiment, therefore, became Hasting's Regiment.

The regiment gained its affiliation with Somerset in 1782 when it became the policy to link a regiment to a county. The association with its commanding officer was also dropped in favour of a number. It became the 13th Somerset Regiment of foot. It acquired the status of a light infantry regiment in 1822 and in 1841, following heroics in Jellalabad, Afghanistan (see seperate entry), the right to use Prince Albert's name. After reforms by Childers in 1881 the numerical system was done away with and it became Prince Albert's Somerset Light Infantry and then in 1920, simply the Somerset Light Infantry. It became amalgamated with the Duke of Cornwall's Light Infantry in 1959 before all the light infantry regiments were merged into one in 1968. It retains its name as the 6th Battalion (Somerset and Cornwall) Light Infantry, a territorial battalion with its headquarters in Taunton.

It has gained 112 battle honours and there have been five recipients of the Victoria Cross. In the nineteenth century it took an active part in campaigns in Burma, Afghanistan and in the Boer War. It took part in both world wars and peacekeeping duties in China, Cyprus and Germany. It had a leading part in the Malayan Emergency at the beginning of the 1950's and was the last regiment to leave India after independence.

William Napier in about 1900 at Rochester with wife Ruth. As Sergeant he received the Victoria Cross for his action in saving Private Benjamin Milnes while under enemy fire (and receiving a wound himself) at Azimghur in Northern India on 6 April 1858. He declined a commission but was promoted to Sergeant Major.

Recipients of the Victoria Cross:

Lieutenant George Albert Cairns
Private Patrick Carlin
Major William Knox Leet
Sergeant William Napier
Private Thomas Henry Sage

Taunton: An A - Z

Somerset Light Infantry: Timeline

1685 Began life as the Earl of Huntingdon's Regiment. Its purpose was to squash the rebellion by the Duke of Monmouth against the Catholic leaning James II.

1688 Becomes known as Hasting's Regiment of Foot under the command of Lieutenant Colonel Ferdinando Hastings. Now allied to the protestant William of Orange.

1689 Fight their first battle at Killekrankie against the Scots.

1695 Now Jacob's Foot under the command of Lieutenant Colonel Sir John Jacob.

1702 Now under the command of the Earl of Barrymore. Took part in the sieges of Venloo, Reuremonde and Chartreuse. (War of Spanish Succession).

1704 In Lisbon and then Gibraltar. Taken for Britain for the first time. First Battle Honour.

1705-6 Capture Barcelona and San Mateo.

1706 Now on horseback as Pearce's Dragoons.

1709 Defeat against the French and Spanish on the River Caya. 300 captured.

1711-28 Garrison duty on Gibraltar.

1743 Now Pulteney's Foot. At the Battle of Dettingen awarded Second battle honour.

1745 Battle of Fontenoy, south west Belgium (War of Austrian Succession).

1746 Battle of Culloden.

1747 Battle of Val, Flanders (War of Austrian Succession).

1751 Regiments ceased to be called by the name of their commander. Pulteny's Foot becomes the 13th Regiment of Foot.

1782 Association with Somerset begins as regiments are now linked to a county. Becomes the 13th Somerset Regiment of Foot.

1790-1794 Serve in the West Indies.

1801 Take part in the Battle at Aboukir Bay (Egypt) where Napoleon is defeated. 'Sphinx' and 'Egypt' are added to colours.

1808 Capture Martenique from the French. Added to battle honours.

1809 Guadeloupe captured from the French.

1813-15 Serve in the American War in support of Canada versus the Unites States.

1822 Becomes the 13th Light Infantry.

1823. Begin service in India.

1824-6 First Burmese War. Awarded battle honour.

1838-42 Serve in Afghan War. Distinguished themselves in an assault on Ghunzee and Jellalabad. More battle honours and takes the name of Prince Albert's Light Infantry.

1851-5 Another spell in Gibraltar.

1855 Awarded battle honours at Sevastapol in the Crimea.

1857 Take a minor role in the Indian Rebellion.

1858 A second battalion is raised.

1877-8 First battalion fight in the 9th Kaffir War.

1878-9 Zulu War. Victoria Cross is won by Major William Knox-Leet and another battle honour is awarded.

1885-7 Third Burmese War fought by the second battalion.

1899-1902 Boer War. Another battle honour awarded in the Relief of Ladysmith

1908 'Territorial Army and Reserve Forces Act' comes into being. Three volunteer battalions become the 4th and 5th battalions. The 3rd Militia became a Special reserve Unit and the 4th Militia was disbanded.

1914-18 19 battalions are raised. 11 battalions fight through Europe and the middle east. Second Battalion Second Battalion remains in India throughout war.

1919 Take part in the third Afghan war.

1920 Become Somerset Light Infantry.

1939-45 Ten battalions raised. The first battalion based in India fighting on the North West frontier and the Japanese in the Arakan, Burma (1943-4).

1947 2nd battalion perform peace-keeping duties in Austria.

1948 The first battalion are the last to leave India. Two battalions become one.

1951 Peace-keeping duties on the Rhine.

1952-5 The Malayan Emergency.

1956 Anti-tank platoon involved in Suez.

1959 Somerset Light Infantry is amalgamated with the Duke of Cornwall Light Infantry. Becomes the Somerset and Cornwall Light Infantry. The Territorial Army keeps the name of the Somerset Light Infantry.

1968 All Light Infantry regiments are amalgamated into one. The 6th (territorial battalion) retains the name Somerset and Cornwall Light Infantry.

Stevens, Maria

Maria Stevens was the last woman tried for witchcraft at the Castle in 1707. She was acquitted of bewitching Dorothy Reece.

Stonegallows

The origin of the name is not certain. One theory is that it was named after

Large stone representing the Stonegallows, erected to commemorate the millenium.

a large boulder stone near to the gallows. Another, that they were originally a special kind of gallows in the style of Montfaucon near Paris where the uprights of the gallows were made from stone. The amateur Historian (and builder) Edward Jeboult, however, was inclined to think the name derived from the fact that they stood on a *stoned* or main road which was unusual at this time.

The first known execution was in 1624 when three men and a woman were hung for the murder of the curate at Old Cleeve. However, it is possible that the site may have been in use from medieval times.

The site of the gallows was marked with a large stone as part of the millennium celebrations at Bishop's Hull. The inscription reads:

'Taunton's execution site from 1575 until 1810, stood here at the junction of the parishes of Bishop's Hull, Trull and Wilton. In 1615, the parishioners of Bishop's Hull were obliged to rebuild the gallows with timber provided by the parish of Trull. On the 15 April 1801, nine men were hanged together for burglary and theft. The gallows were probably removed in 1814.'

The nine men who were hanged and their crimes (which did not include a single case of murder) were as follows:

Edward Jeffrey, 49 of Chardstock for sheep stealing
William Warry of Chardstock, 49 for sheep stealing.
Robert Weygood of Milverton, 26 for burglary in the house
of G. Hancock.
George Tout (alias Greenslade), 27 of Upton for stealing wheat.
William Tout, 26 of Wiveliscombe for rioting and forcibly
taking bread out of a baker's shop.
John Westcote of Withycombe for rioting and forcibly taking
bread out of a baker's shop.
Robert Deo (alias Williams), 24 for burglary.
Peter Kingdon, 22 born at Withycombe for stealing Heifers.
Michael Day, 46 of Holton for stealing Heifers.

An eyewitness account states how, 'The nice poor fellows were driven from prison to Bishop's Hull in a cart sitting on their coffins. The nine ropes for hanging were suspended from an erected gallows. As the ropes were placed around the necks of the men the cart was drawn away from under them and they were left suspended. The nine men were hanged at once.'

Though they were not all bread rioters as this and some accounts erroneously stated, it is significant that the only two of the nine men who denied their guilt were William Tout and John Westcote who were convicted of stealing bread. They had broken into the house of the baker Richard Griffey in Old Cleeve on 30 March 1801 and stole 15 loaves of bread. 'of the value of one pound two shillings and sixpence.' They had, in fact, left some money for the bread, though the amount they thought it should be worth rather than the amount being asked. The price of bread was a contentious issue. There had been bread riots at regular intervals throughout the country in the 18th century and the worst of these were in 1795 and 1801. Bread was a staple diet of the working man so having no bread meant having no food. Harvested grain had traditionally been brought to town and sold at a price regulated by custom and tradition. The baker's produced the bread, again at regulated prices. It was, essentially, a local arrangement. However, with the growth of the market economy and the commercialisation of farming in the 18th century, the farmer's began behaving differently, hoarding the grain in times of shortage so that they might sell later when prices were dear or exporting out of their locality to areas of the country where they might receive a better price. This was exacerbated in poor years of harvest.

The judge, though, when summing up the cases of the nine men had little sympathy. In his view, when William Tout and John Westcote paid their own price for the bread it was 'in fact the same as if they had taken it without paying anything, because no person has a right to fix the price and take another the same as if they had taken an others property.' After the jury had found the two men guilty he had no hesitation in condemning them to the gallows.

139

Pick-pocketing ceased to be punishable by death in 1808, but it was not until the 1830's that sheep stealing and burglary were removed from the list of capital offences. By 1838, only treason, murder and attempted murder were capital offences (on land).

There were, it is believed, two more hangings at Stonegallows after this. The first was that of James Taylor, 23, on April 10, 1809 for shooting John Dyer and wounding another man. The last hanging is believed to be that of 18 year old Thomas Gage, alias Tarr, in 1810 for the murder of Elizabeth Stylings of Goathurst.

Public hangings were usually well attended and were looked on by many as a form of entertainment. In F. T. Elworth's Word Book of West Somerset he relates how a young couple arranged their marriage around a hanging 'so they may be gwain there fust, vor a bit of a spree.'

In January 1814 a letter was sent to the editor of the Taunton Courier signed by 'An inhabitant of Bishop's Hull.' He suggested that the gibbet at Stonegallows should be removed 'As no possible public utility can be answered by this permanent erection, which the trivial expense of a temporary one would not equally afford, it is difficult to conceive why an object should be thus preserved, which is so painfully uncongenial, in the reflections to which it gives rise, with the soothing features of the surrounding scenery.'

We do not know how influential this letter had been but it appears that the gallows were removed soon after.

Tangier

The origin of the name Tangier, the area to the west of the Castle, is not clear. One theory is that it has its origins in the civil war in Taunton. In 1665 Sir John Warre was ordered to recruit soldiers from a fractious Taunton. He marched 120 men to Plymouth bound for the garrison in Tangier, held by the English from 1661 to 1684 when it was returned to Morocco.

Another possibility is that the name originated from the time of the Monmouth Rebellion, following the debacle at the Battle of Sedgemoor. Colonel Percy Kirke was colonel of one of the Tangier regiments and in 1682 was appointed Governor of Tangier and Colonel of the Old Tangier Regiment. On his return to England his 'Lambs' (from the badge they wore) took part in the battle of Sedgemoor under the command of Lord Feversham. Kirke brought prisoners and wounded into Taunton where 19 were hanged. Though some of the atrocities claimed for Kirke are now known to have been exaggerated, the events surrounding that period lived long in the memory and the association of Kirke and his Tangier regiment with Taunton has often been made.

Taunton Cabinet

The Taunton Cabinet was made for the great exhibition of 1851 by John Stevens, cabinet maker. It still survives and is normally exhibited in the County Museum. It was followed by the Taunton Sideboard in 1862, made for the International Exhibition, though its whereabouts, if it has survived, are unknown.

Taunton Cider

For many years the Taunton Cider Company based in Norton Fitzwarren, just outside Taunton, was an important local employer. With its nationally represented products of cider and perry along with some high profile television advertising, it helped put Taunton 'on the map.'

The origins of Taunton Cider lay in the Rectory at Heathfield a few miles to the west of Taunton, first under the care of the Reverend Thomas Cornish and then under the direction of the Spurway family. By 1910, under the management of Reverend Spurway, the Heathfield Rectory was producing 5,000 gallons of cider a year.

However, within two years the Reverend Spurway became ill. His

Taunton Cider, about 1930

successor at the Rectory was not interested in continuing his cider business. A local builder, William Vickery, bought the orchards and some of the equipment and employed the services of the assistant gardener of the Rectory at the new premises in Norton Fitzwarren. This was later sold to George Pallet. He had moved to Norton Fitzwarren at the beginning of the First World War having sold a bottled food and drink business, which had included cider-making.

When finances proved difficult after the end of the war, Pallet sought the help of a London accountant named Frank Rowley. He put the business onto a sounder footing and in 1921 Taunton Cider became a limited company, with Rowley as chairman and Riley as managing director.

Rowley used his influence as an accountant to many London theatre companies and introduced cider into a number of the theatre bars in London. In 1927 the Oakhill Brewery suffered a fire and its cider-making facilities were destroyed. It did not replace them and Rowley persuaded them to accept the supply of cider from Taunton Cider to their tied houses. In addition, Taunton Cider also hired an agent who, by 1939, had established sales of their cider to 350 public houses.

Following the war, growth was spurred by the acquisition of the Quantock Vale Cider Company and an agreement to supply to the tied houses of their former owners, Starkey, Knight and Ford.

Further growth came after the decision of Courage and Whitbread to supply its chain of public houses with cider from Taunton Cider. Other brewers with tied houses followed suit and, by 1970, Taunton Cider was making nearly five million gallons of cider a year.

The business developed again when Guinness became a shareholder at Taunton Cider in 1971 and the marketing emphasis was shifted to exploit the brands of Autumn Gold and the newly developed Diamond White and Dry Blackthorn products. Guinness was no longer a shareholder after 1985 but the marketing emphasis continued. By 1991, profit was £10.5 million pounds on a turnover of £109.4 million pounds and there were 451 people employed. A successful management buy out was completed in May 1991 and soon after it became a public company. The following year, profits increased to £17.08 million pounds and the number of employees rose to 512.

In November 1995 it was taken over by Matthew Clark. The Norton Fitzwarren operation was ended by March 1996. They were relocated to a rented warehouse near Bristol. Their main distribution partner, Langdon's, was side lined, a new computer system was introduced and the sales and marketing budgets were reduced. Three years later after a period of poor sales, the company was sold to the American owned Canandaigua. While the former Taunton Cider Company failed, its main competitor through the years, Bulmers, prospered.

Robert Holder puts it succinctly in his book, *Taunton Cider and the Langdons*: 'Ultimately, the real losers were the people of Taunton, and especially those who worked in Norton Fitzwarren at Taunton Cider PLC.'

Taunton Invasion Committee

The Taunton Invasion Committee was set up during the Second World War, in case of invasion by Germany. Its records were known as the 'Black Book'. If an invasion took place 400 civilians would be mobilised into action for defence work by the Garrison Commander, the senior military officer in the town. Trees would be felled, trenches and weapons pits would be dug, materials would be gathered together for an emergency bridge over the Tone should the existing bridge be destroyed. A Civil Defence Ambulance Service and an Emergency Hospital Service would take care of any casualties. Bishop Fox's School for girls in Kingston Road (now a housing estate), would be first in line as an emergency hospital. There were 48 food packs after which the Women's Voluntary Service would take charge of feeding the Home Guard. Short range wireless stations were set up in case of communications being severed. In all there were 48 members of the invasion committee.

Taunton, Lord (1798 - 1869)

When Henry Labouchere lost his seat as an MP in the election of 1859 he became the first Lord Taunton

He was born at Over Stowey and was MP for Michael Borough as a Whig in 1826. He moved to the Taunton seat in 1830 and was to retain the seat until 1859 when he was elevated to the House of Lords. His election triumphs included one Benjamin Disraeli who unsuccessfully contested the seat in 1835.

He saw office as Civil Lord of the Admiralty, Master of the Mint, Privy Councillor, Vice President and President of the Board of Trade, Under Secretary of State for War and the Colonies and Chief Secretary for Ireland.

He married Frances Baring of the Barings Bank in 1840. She died in 1850 leaving him one daughter. He married again to Mary Howard (who could trace her lineage back to Catherine Howard), in 1852. They had two daughters together. Without a son, his title did not carry on after him. He was a wealthy man who developed the Quantock Lodge (near Over Stowey) and bought much of the surrounding land. Quantock Lodge was to be a summer residence to house his own and his wife's art collection. He was also the moving force behind the building of the site for what we now know as King's College. He formed a company called the Taunton College School Company Limited in November 1866 with capital of £12,500 to accommodate the school at the Municipal Buildings in Corporation Street, whose pupil numbers had greatly increased. He also made available an interest free loan of £1,000. However, he died, in 1869, before he could see its completion, aged 71.

Taunton (Massachusetts)
The sister town of Taunton, Somerset.

Taunton Green, Massachusetts

By 1900 Taunton, Massachusetts population had outstripped its namesake. This remained the case until recent times. Now the two Taunton's are remarkably similar in their population size. There were 55,976 in Taunton, Massachusetts as of the 2000 census as opposed to 53,290 in the Taunton, Somerset census of 2001.

Other similarities are that they are both the administrative centres of their respective counties (Somerset and Bristol County), they both have a Mayor, and they both have in the past been a centre of dissent and political machinations.

Taunton, Massachusetts was the first town in America where a woman, Elizabeth Pole, was credited with its founding. One of the founders of the Declaration of Independence, Robert Treat Paine was a resident and part of King Phillip's War and part of the American Civil War was fought around Taunton, as Taunton Somerset had an important role in the English Civil War. Also, like its counterpart, it has a healthy rainfall. In October 2005 in Taunton, Massachusetts there were nine inches of rain causing 2000 residents to be evacuated. (In fact its average yearly rainfall is 49 inches as against 35 inches in Taunton, Somerset).

As one would expect, many of the town settlers were from Taunton, Somerset and it is from this that derives its name, 'in honour and love to our dear native country', when it was founded in 1637. The land had formerly belonged to the

St Mary's Church, Taunton, Masachusetts.

native Wampanoags and the area was known as Cohanet. It was re incorporated as a city on May 11, 1864.

The main river is called Taunton River. Its railway was established in 1838, four years earlier than in Taunton, Somerset. Its economy was based on shipbuilding and on making products from silver. It made the medals for the 1996 summer Olympics and is sometimes known as the 'Silver City'. It is the headquarters of various leading corporations.

The Taunton Public Library was opened in 1903, two years before its English counterpart in Corporation Street. The city square is known as Taunton Green. It is sometimes known as 'Christmas City' because of the stunning display of Christmas lights and events.

During the Second World War, on 3 July 1941, a mobile canteen was presented in Vivary Park to Taunton, Somerset, 'With the best wishes of your namesake in America.'

Taunton School

Founded as the West of England and Dissenters' Proprietary School, or Independent College, in 1847.

The school came into being as a result of a desire for better education for Nonconformists who were thought to be looked down on by Church of England boys. A central role was

played by Rev Henry Addiscott and Rev Henry Quick. Teachers and other school staff were to be from the Protestant Dissenting Community and the curriculum was to be wide and varied. The school was funded by the sale of 800 shares at £10.00 each. A group of four houses were rented at Stepswater in Wellington at £180 per annum.

The school was immediately successful and a school room and a day room was hurriedly commissioned. By 1849 there were 118 pupils. The first headmaster of the school was Dr. Bewglass, an Irishman of high academic achievement. However, there was an opinion that he was not enough of a disciplinarian and he resigned in 1854. He was replaced by the Rev. Thomas Clarke of Rotherham. He inherited the headship during a period of high inflation and a smallpox epidemic and was not able to reverse a decline in numbers. He, in turn, was replaced by W. H. Griffiths in 1857. He was able to increase the numbers and put the school back into profit.

A site for a new school was eventually settled on at Fairwater, 'situated one mile from the Market Place, on the Staplegrove Road.' The site was purchased from Dr. William Gillet in 1865. It was built between 1867 and 1870 by Joseph James of London in the Gothic style, dominated by a 50 ft tower in the centre. The grey stone was supplied from the Mendips. Griffiths saw them through the move to the new school and remained as head until 1880 when he resigned on health grounds after 23 years service.

Mr Avebury succeeded him and stayed until 1894. He was very popular and when he resigned and set up a new school at Blackheath in London he took a good number of pupils and staff with him so that the new headmaster inherited a school with just 54 senior boys and 7 juniors. He was not able to rejuvenate the school and it was not until the headship of a Dr. Whittaker that the school once again became successful. He quickly doubled the numbers and by 1902 there were 210 pupils. Many of the buildings that are familiar today date from his time at the school. One of the most notable examples is the chapel, by Sir Frank Wills, which was added in 1906, the gift of Lord Winterstoke. The school changed its name to Taunton School in 1899. When he retired in 1922 the school had 728 pupils.

Weirfield School was Established in 1879. It was intended to educate the sisters of boys at Taunton School, nearby.

Weirfield School for Girls, Taunton.

Principal: : : MRS. LOVEDAY.

When Mrs Loveday, the principal of Weirfield, was forced to give up through illness, a Miss Barford and a Miss Bidder took on the mantle of the school and the numbers quadrupled to 165 within ten years.

In 1976 it merged with the senior part of Taunton School and Taunton School thus became a co-educational School. With the sale of the Weirfield site the girls junior school was incorporated into Taunton School with the addition of a new building in 1993.

Taunton Stop Line

In case of invasion by Germany during the Second World War a 'stop line' was built between Highbridge in the north and Seaton in the south.

The 'line' followed waterways and railways for almost 50 miles. This was accompanied by obstacles and blocks on all roads and railways. Following a meeting at County Hall in June 1940 between the builders, Stansell and Sons and the Military, 355

Pillbox on Taunton Stop Line

pillboxes were built with gun emplacements at intervals between. The pillboxes were built at great speed by using civilian labour and the pioneer corps.

An invasion was expected at any time. On 7 September there was an invasion scare and the swing bridges over the canal were hastily dismantled. When the scare was over, several prefabricated bridges were built to aid the farmers in taking their cows for milking. Once built they were disguised and, as far as possible, they were blended in with their surroundings. The aqueduct at Creech was a perfect anti-tank obstacle. A company of the second Somerset B Battalion (Taunton) manned the line between Thornfalcon and Creech St Michael.

About 280 pillboxes survive in varying conditions with gun emplacements every few hundred yards. It has been dubbed 'the Hadrians's Wall of the Twentieth Century. '

The seven year Defence of Britain Project which involved an army of about 600 volunteers recording Britain's defences has shown that by the middle of 1941, Britain had a thorough network of defences in place and that the Taunton Stop Line was a key component of this.

A 'Starfish' or decoy site was built near Bradford on Tone.

Taunton Time

Until the middle of the nineteenth century all communities set their clocks to local time. When a traveller moved eastward or westward he or she simply adjusted their watches when they arrived in each new town. With the coming of the railway and the introduction of the railway timetable and the telegraph, all this changed. They needed one agreed time they could rely on. The standard adopted was that of Greenwich Observatory, which became the standard for the world. Taunton was 12 minutes behind. In January 1848 the clocks were moved forward 12 minutes to synchronise with Green-wich Mean Time.

James Lackington

Temple Methodist Church

The Temple Methodist Church was built by James Lackington who's story is worth recording.

He was born in Wellington in 1746 the son of a drunken shoemaker and weaver's daughter. At the age of ten he became an itinerant pie-seller in order to help support his mother and eleven brothers and sisters. He was apprenticed to a Taunton shoemaker at the age of 14 and attended the Methodist assembly of David Burford in Blackboy Lane in Taunton. This is where a love of reading began. After a time in Bristol, where he kept up his Methodist interests, he moved to London and eventually took a shop in Featherstone Street as a master shoe-maker. He soon, however, began selling books in his shop and with the aid of a £5.00 loan from a Wesleyan fund and thrift and hard work built up a stock worth £25.00. He was able to give up shoe-making and moved to new premises nearer the City in Chiswell Street. However, he and his wife, Nancy, both caught fever. Nancy died. He survived and married Dorcas Turton in 1776, who had helped nurse him through his fever. 'I repaired the loss of one very valuable woman by the acquisition of another still more valuable.', he said. This comment may be a clue to his later success, for Dorcas loved books and was helpful in the business.

He adopted a trading policy whereby he refused to accept credit, which was unusual at that time and kept his margins very tight. He also brought publishers remainders and

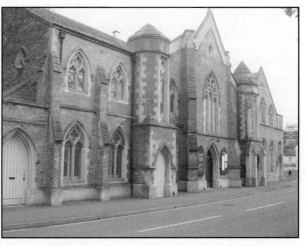

whole libraries and then sold them on cheaply. He became very successful and, in 1789 he moved to a large shop in Finsbury Square which he called the Temple of the Muses. It had a frontage which was 1400 feet long and, in the centre of the shop, an enormous circular counter around which, it was said, a coach and horses could be driven. By 1791 his annual profit was £4,000.

He retired in 1804 and built a Methodist Chapel at Alveston near Bristol. In 1806 he moved to Taunton and bought some land called Poole Wall (near Shuttern) where he began to build another chapel. A memorandum in a bottle under the foundations stone read: 'This chapel was begun in 1808, and built at the sole expense of James Lackington, a local preacher in connection of the Methodists belonging to the late Rev. Mr John Wesley.'

It was Lackington's intention that the Methodists worshipping at the Octagon in Middle Street would move into the new chapel, called the Temple after his bookshop. They were there at its opening but not for long. There was a disagreement between Lackington and the Octagon brethren. The Kilhamites, a breakaway Methodist group started by Alexander Kilham in 1795, were in the town at the time and were accepted by Lackington instead. Again, however, there was disagreement. Lackington made another approach to the Octagon Methodists but they stated that they would only return if they were able to purchase the Temple Chapel outright. They bought it for £1,050, about a third of the price it cost to build, and moved there in 1812.

Lackington built another chapel in Budleigh Salterton in Devon, again called the Temple, and died there in 1815.

His motto, which he put on the side of his carriage was, 'Small profits do great things.'

A new facade was added to the Temple Methodist Church in 1846. A school was added in 1866 and the chapel was rebuilt in 1869.

Theatre

James Biggs, a comedian, opened the first permanent theatre in East Reach in 1786. It was described by Toulmin in his History of Taunton as 'small but neat'. Until this time Taunton was visited by touring theatres who would perform at Castle Green or in one of the local pubs.

In 1800 a theatre was opened in Silver Street, adjoining the Baptist Chapel, by Henry Lee. He was also the manager and apparently a good actor. The first performance was of a favourite play of the time, Heir at Law, on the 27 March. The following is taken from the Somersetshire Directory of 1840:

'In Silver Street we come first to the Theatre, a shabby looking place outside, but within fitted up in a very graceful and comfortable style, and having an excellent company on the stage, though we regret to say, generally a very thin one in the other parts of the house.'

The Taunton Courier of the 6 February 1839 describes a performance by Charles Keane (weslyan son) as Sir Edward Mortimer in The Iron Chest 'to an over-flowing house.' He 'received form the audience the habitual manifestation of respect for his great histrionic talent. At the conclusion of the play Mr Keane was loudly called for, and presenting himself acknowledged his thankfulness for the favour he had experienced on that his first appearance on the Taunton boards.' He tells the audience that he is unable to perform there again before he departs for America but the sailing time is altered and a fortnight later he appears in Hamlet and the Taunton Courier of 20 February proclaims: 'That gentleman's impersonation of Hamlet has justly been considered the best test of his talents; and having amply satisfied the most fastidious judges of the dramatic art, by his masterly delineation of a character in which thousands have failed, and very

few have succeeded, it was the equal surprise and admiration that Mr Keane was found entitled to share in the glories that had enreathed the brows of his most distinguished predecessors...'

The Silver Street Theatre was demolished in 1846.

The Brewhouse Theatre in Taunton, opened on 28th March 1977

The Assembly rooms

at the London Hotel (later the County Hotel) were opened in 1849 and was used for staging theatre as well as other events. Two of the Taunton cinemas also had good stage facilities. The Lyceum, which opened in 1913 had six dressing rooms with a 30 ft. proscenium and a fly tower and could seat over 500. Sarah Bernhardt, Vesta Tilley and Hillaire Belloc are all known to have performed there. The Gaumont opened in 1932 in Corporation Street and had eight dressing rooms, a 52 ft. wide proscenium, a fly tower and could seat over 1,400. The Taunton Amateur Operatic Society's experience is typical. Before the war it held its productions at the London Hotel Assembly Rooms. After the war productions were shared between here (later named The Empire and then the County Theatre), and the Lyceum. From 1936 until after the war they were produced at the Gaumont, until the closing of the cinema in 1981, when they moved to the Brewhouse.

The Brewhouse opened on 28 March 1977 with a performance of Alan Ayckbourn's *The Norman Conquest* starring a young David Jason. The main auditorium has 350 seats. Originally, a much larger theatre was planned for. This now may become a reality with a proposal to develop the theatre as part of 'Project Taunton', a scheme to develop the town, where it is hoped seating capacity will be increased to above 600.

The Taunton Amateur Operatic Society apart, of local theatre groups, the Taunton Thespians have been going the longest, since 1927. The Wayfarers were established in 1967.

Tomacelli, Pierro

He was Archdeacon of Taunton before his election as Pope Boniface XI in 1389.

Toulmin, Joshua (1740 -1815)

Joshua Toulmin was a radical minister whose lasting legacy is the first comprehensive history of Taunton.

He was born and educated in London, first at St Paul's School and then at the Dissenting Academy in Wellclose Square.

He was then appointed to the Presbyterian Minister at Colyton in Devon. He converted to the Baptists and, in particular, to the idea of adult baptism (or believer's baptism) rather than infant baptism. In 1765, still only 25, he became the Baptist Minister at Mary Street Unitarian Chapel in Taunton where he remained for the next 39 years. He was also a teacher and a prolific author, publishing over 60 seperate works.

His great legacy to Taunton was the publication of the first History of Taunton in 1791, a lengthy and detailed history of Taunton which remains a valuable source of reference. The previous year he had conducted a census of Taunton, walking around each dwelling, at a time when population estimates were notoriously inaccurate. He counted nearly 5,500 'within the area ringed by the turnpike gates.'

Several of his tracts were in support of the American (1775-1783) and French (1787-1790) revolutions. This led him to being the subject of insults in the street, broken windows and the burning of an effigy of Thomas Paine outside his door.

He married Jane Smith at the age of 24. Of their twelve children only five survived. The drowning of his daughter, Jane, near Sidmouth on 15 April 1798, must have affected him deeply, though he bore it stoically as the poet Samuel Taylor Coleridge related. He walked eleven miles into Taunton from Nether Stowey to perform the service on behalf of Dr. Toulmin. He suffered it, he said 'like the true practical Christian, - there is indeed a tear in his eye, but that eye is lifted up to the heavenly father.'

He underwent a further religious conversion to the Unitarian Church and in 1804 he moved to Birmingham to become a Unitarian Minister. He died on 23 July 1815, aged 75.

Trams

Tram in Fore Street about 1906.

The longest name and one of the shortest routes in the country.

Electric trams ran in Taunton between 1901 and 1922.

'The Taunton and West Somerset Electric Railways and Tramways Company' was shortened to 'The Taunton Electric Traction Company Ltd.' in 1903 as the earlier ambitious schemes to cover much of West Somerset did not become realised.

It stuttered into operation in 1901 after a false start in 1897. The original line beginning from a depot in East Reach, crossed Gray's Road, Haydon Road, Silver Street, Fore Street, North Street, Bridge Street and Belvedere Road until it reached its northern terminus in Station Road. The track was 3ft 6in narrow gauge.

A complete refurbishment of the track, which was considered to have been poorly laid, took place in 1905. Six new single deck tramcars were purchased and the old cars sold to Leamington and Warwick Tram Railway and, in one case, to Llandudno and Colwyn Bay Railway.

There was an extension to a new terminus in Kingston Road at Salisbury Street in 1909.

The tramway closed in 1921. The immediate cause was an argument over electricity prices which resulted in the power being switched off.

Nine of the overhead poles still remain in Greenway Crescent and are used for Street Lighting. A further pole carries electrical wires in the centre of Bishops Lydeard.

Former overhead tram pole still in use carrying electrical wires at Bishops Lydeard

Trenchard, Hugh Montague, GCM OM GCVO DSO (1873-1956)

Born in Taunton, he has been described as the 'father of the Royal Air Force.'

Born at Windsor Lodge in Taunton, the third child of Henry and Georgina Tower, he was good at games though a poor scholar. His father, who was a solicitor, went bankrupt when he was 16, so he was dependent on his relatives to fund the remainder of his education. He failed entrance exams twice, for Dartmouth Royal Naval College and Woolwich Academy, before scraping into the army at his third attempt.

However, his horsemanship impressed. He was commissioned to the Royal Scots Fusiliers in 1893 to serve in South Africa.

Unfortunately, in 1900, he was shot, and received an injury to his lung and spine and sent home an invalid.

Remarkably, while convalescing in Switzerland, his spine was 'fixed' bizarrely by a bad crash while bobsleighing on the Cresta Run (he had taken it up through boredom). He was able to walk with the aid of sticks and return to South Africa in May 1901. In 1906, after serving in Nigeria, he received a DSO.

In 1913 he learned to fly at Thomas Sopwith's Flying School after passing a course that only involved 64 minutes of flying time. At 39 he was only a year short of being disqualified as a pilot due to his age. He transferred to the Royal Flying Corps, at this time a branch of the army, where he earned the nickname 'Boom' because of his loud speaking voice.

By August 1915 he had become General Officer Commander of the Royal Flying Corps in France. He became Chief of Staff of the newly formed Air Council in January 1918. He helped form the RAF from the RFC's merger with the Royal Naval Air Service in April 1918, though he resigned just before the official date of the merger after an argument with Lord Rothermere. In June, he turned his attention to organising the bombing of strategic targets in Germany.

Reappointed as Chief of Staff by Winston Churchill in 1919, he founded a training college for air cadets and introduced short-service commissions to provide a pool of trained air service personnel. He married Katherine Boyle at St Margaret's Church in Westminster in July 1920. He was to keep his position as Chief of Staff until 1927 when he was made first Marshall of the RAF. He retired two years later. He was created a Baron in 1930 and appointed commissioner of the Metropolitan Police in 1931. He made some important reforms including the establishment of the Police Training College at Hendon.

In 1936 he was made a Viscount and became a chairman of the United Africa Company. The RAF shrunk considerably in size after the First World War to his dismay and he took every opportunity to remark about the unpreparedness of the Air Force. He toured the airfields giving advice and encouragement to pilots during the Second World War, and continued to formulate ideas about the air force after the war. Following his death on 10 February 1956 he was buried in the Battle of Britain Chapel in Westminster.

Trevelyan, Sir Charles Edward (1807-1886)

Born in Taunton, the son of George Trevelyan, the Archdeacon of Taunton, and Harriet Neave, he is widely regarded as the founder of the modern civil service.

He was educated at Taunton Grammar School, Charterhouse and Haileybury, a private school in Herefordshire. He was good at languages and entered into the East India Company's Bengal Civil Service as a writer in 1826. In 1827 he was appointed the assistant to Sir Charles Theophilus Metcalfe, the Commissioner of Delhi. He devoted himself to improving the conditions of the Indian population and was instrumental in the abolition of transit duties which had hitherto hindered trade in India. He also contributed some of his own money to constructing a broad street in a new suburb of Delhi which became known as Trevelyanpur. He went to Calcutta as deputy secretary to the government in 1831 and in 1834 he married Hannah Moore, sister of Lord McCauley.

Before his return to England in 1837, he was particularly influential in the field of education and was largely responsible for the adoption of a policy of the teaching of European science and literature to the indigenous population. For 19 years, from 1840, he was assistant secretary to the treasury. As a result, he was in charge of the administration of the government relief to victims of the Irish famine. His sympathetic attitude to the indigenous population of India did not extend to Ireland and the famine, where he proved to be cold-hearted and uncompassionate. He described the famine as, 'a mechanism for reducing surplus population', and 'The judgement of god reflecting the moral evil of the selfish, perverse and turbulent character of the people.' The relief that was given under his direction was too little, too slow and inefficient. He refused to interfere with the policy of exporting grain from Ireland while the population starved, was against creating jobs through railway construction and Russell's plan to distribute 50,000 seeds to tenants. In the autumn of 1857 he ended government aid declaring that the famine was over. In the April of the following year he received a Knighthood.

In 1853 he headed an inquiry into the improvement of the Civil Service. Together with Lord Northcote, a report on 'The Organisation of the Permanent Civil Service' led to the introduction of competitive examinations to make the service a more professional body. To many he is considered the father of the modern civil service. In Trollope's novel, The Three Clerks (1858), Trevelyan is portrayed by Sir Geoffrey Hardlines.

After the Indian Uprising of 1857 he returned to India in 1858 as Governor of Madras where he undertook some important reforms, especially in the police. He was recalled from India for a time following the release of some government information that was considered subversive. After another return as finance minister between 1862 and 1865 he devoted himself to making reforms in the army particularly with regard to the purchase of army commissions. In later years he was also involved in various charitable enterprises and social causes. He died in June 1886.

Tudor House, Fore Street

Thought to be the oldest private building in Taunton. It was rebuilt in the 1550's under the ownership of Sir William Portman and the tenancy of Thomas Trowbridge. Before that it was owned by the Marchaunt family. The oldest parts of the building date back to the middle of the 14th century. It was the West Somerset Stores between 1871 and 1906 and Halliday's Antique Shop between 1909 and 1946. In recent times it has been a restaurant and a pub and is currently a Coffee House.

Turnpike Trustees

Before the advent of the canal and the train, carrying goods and people by coach was an important means of transport. Wheeled traffic did not become common until the sixteenth century. An act was passed in parliament in 1555 in which the responsibility for the upkeep of roads was placed on the parish. Each parish elected two 'Waywardens'. All householders were to provide four days labour for the upkeep of their road. This was later increased to six days. Though this worked reasonably well at local level this was not so for main roads, which the parish had little interest in. Local responsibility within towns in many cases passed to the borough council or local health board but this was only a partial solution to the problems of poor roads. As traffic increased with the growth of manufacturing and an increase in the transportation of goods and materials in the 18th century there came into being the Turnpike Trusts, made lawful by individual acts of parliament. They were empowered to collect tolls at gates or turnpikes for the upkeep of existing roads or the building of new ones. It did not apply to those on foot or soldiers or Royal Mail Coaches.

When Taunton applied for a turnpike act it was opposed by Humphrey Sydenham, the MP for Exeter who said that the roads around Taunton were in good repair. However, Thomas Prowse MP countered that the roads were in such a bad state of repair that it would be easier to make them into canals rather than to make them into roads for carriages.

The act was passed in 1752. Roads that were turnpiked included Taunton to Tricky Warren, Taunton to Buncombe Hill via Kingston St Mary, the terminus quaintly described as being 'the corner of Master Cole's Wall in the parish of Broomfield' and Taunton to Yard's Barn - from Rowbarton and along Cheddon Road. In 1765 a new act was passed extending to several of the roads adjoining Taunton. A further act in 1788 altered slightly the qualification required to become a trustee, equalised the toll rates and ring-fenced some of the toll money to repairing the footways in the centre of Taunton. Joshua Toulmin, who wrote his History of Taunton shortly after this, enthused about the latter alteration to the act. A fourth act in 1799 related mainly to the extension of the some of the tolls and to the widening of the road from Shoreditch to Holway Lane (now South Street). An act of 1817 united all the trusts into one and authorised a new road from Bishop's Hull to Rumwell and from the village of Chilson to Wellington. It also gave permission for the demolition of several of the houses in East Street and the High Street to enable improvements to the roads within the centre of the town.

There were tolls at Shuttern, Spittle (St Margaret's Almshouses), The George Inn (at the junction of Staplegrove Road and Bridge Street), Rowbarton, New Cross Lane (now Holway Avenue), Holway and, it is believed, a further one at Cann Street. As the town expanded there were protests that the tolls were too close to the town. They were eventually moved outside the borough. Tarmacadam came in 1831. In 1838 the trust built a new road along the Wellington Road and, in 1848, Park Street. Some roads were built privately such as Alma Street and Haines Hill. In 1876, responsibility for the roads passed from the Turnpike Trust to the Highway Board.

United Reformed Church

The first building was Paul's Meeting House and was built in about 1672, George Newton was its first minister and it soon attracted a large congregation. However, its path was not smooth. On Mayor Timewell's instruction in 1683 the doors were broken and the building sacked and it was closed for worship. There were two attempts to turn it into a workhouse.

However, following the Glorious Revolution which brought William of Orange to the throne, and the Act of Toleration of 1689, it was reopened.

The present building was erected in 1797.

Victoria Rooms, The Parade

First built as the New Market House in 1821, according to Toulmin, 'for the purpose of affording additional accommodations to the increased business of the market' . The stone was laid on 28 February by Charles Tynte , Esq. The architect was William Burgess of Exeter and the builder was Thomas Norman of Taunton. In 1822 several of the stalls that traded from the existing market house and from the Parade moved to the New Market House. It later became the Victoria Rooms and then the Town Hall. For a time it housed the School of Art which moved there in 1889 from Bath Place until a purpose built School of Art was built in Corporation Street to where it moved in 1907.

Vivary Park

Two ponds, or vivaria (hence the name), were established by 1208, to supply the Castle and, occasionally, the Royal Household. These, though, were no ordinary ponds. They were more akin to a modern fish farm. It is likely that the larger one covered part of what is now the golf course while the smaller one was in the confines of the present day park. By the 1360's the fish ponds covered at least 70 acres.

Since 1851 the park has hosted many annual public events including the annual Flower Show. In the early years time this was by the permission of the Kinglake family who lived at Wilton House. The land was purchased in 1894 for £3,569. The park was laid out in 1895 along with the bandstand and gates. The fountain was built with funds left over from the celebrations for the coronation of Edward VII as a memorial to Queen Victoria and opened in 1907. The war me-

morial, paid for by public subscription, was unveiled on 26 March 1922. It lists the names of 464 soldiers who lost their life in the first world war. The Putting Green was opened in 1927 followed by the Golf Course in 1928.

A boating pond and the beds of roses around the memorial were added in the 1960's. The model railway track was opened in 1979 and a year later the playground next to the tennis courts. The park has well developed trees and flowers and extensive lawns dividing it into roughly two wide open spaces, a tributary to the river Tone and a lake. It is a haven for birds and the Flower Show has developed over the years to be known as the Chelsea of the West.

In 2001 and 2002 the park underwent a program of restoration with a £750,000 grant from the Heritage Lottery Fund and Taunton Deane Borough Council. It was opened by the Queen on 2 May 2002, her Jubilee Year.

Warbeck, Perkin

Perkin Warbeck made an abortive attempt to claim the throne from Henry VII before being captured and brought to Taunton Castle.

He claimed to be the missing son of Edward V1 (Richard of Shrewsbury), the youngest of the two princes in the tower and to therefore have a claim to the throne of Henry VII. He was, in fact, Flemish born and the son of a weaver though he was curiously recognised as Richard of Shrewsbury by Margaret of Burgundy, Edward VI's sister.

In 1490 he landed in Ireland hoping to garner support for his claim. However, little was forthcoming. On his return to France, he gained the support of Edward IV's sister, Margaret of Burgundy. She funded a small army which landed at Deal in Kent on 3 July 1495. His army, though, was routed and he fled, first to Ireland, and then to Scotland, where he was welcomed by James IV and married his cousin, Lady Catherine Gordon. However, the following year the King expelled him and he went once more to Ireland.

On 7 September 1497 he landed in Cornwall with an army intending to march on London. He was declared Richard IV on Bodmin Moor and with an army of 6,000 men proceeded first to Exeter and then to Taunton. On the approach of the Royalist army under the command of Lord Daubeney, he fled to Hampshire taking 60 followers with him. Henry VII entered Taunton on 4 October 1497. Warbeck's army surrendered and the ringleaders were either executed or fined. Warbeck himself was captured at Beaulieu in Hampshire and brought back to Taunton Castle where he admitted that he was only a weaver's son.

He was sent to the Tower of London where he was paraded through the streets on horseback. He tried to escape the tower in 1499 with the Earl of Warwick, who had a genuine claim to the throne. However, he was captured on the 23 November and was drawn on a hurdle from the tower to Tyburn where he read out a confession before he was hanged.

One consequence was the placing of Henry VII's coat of arms over the Castle's Gatehouse and there they remain to this day.

Weirfield School (see Taunton School)

Wesley, John (1703-1791)
John Wesley visited Taunton a number of times between 1743 and 1789.

He kept a diary of his visits which the following extracts show, did not often pass without controversy.

Friday 26 August 1743
'I set out for Cornwall. In the evening I preached at the cross in Taunton, on, "the Kingdom of God is not meat and drink; but righteousness, and peace, and joy in the Holy Ghost." A poor man had posted himself behind, in order to make some disturbance: But the time was not come; the zealous wretches who "deny the Lord that brought them," had not stirred up the people. Many cried out, "Throw down that rascal there: knock him down: beat out his brains." So that I was obliged to entreat him more than once, or he would have been but roughly handled.'

Thursday 22 September 1743
'.....rode on to Taunton, where we were gladly received by a little company of our brethren from Bristol. I had designed to preach in the yard of our inn, but before I had named my text, having uttered only two words, "Jesus Christ," a tradesman of the town (who it seems was Mayor elect) made so much noise and uproar, that we thought it best give him ground. But many of the people followed me up into a large room, where I preached unto them Jesus.'

However, things began to improve, though it took a long time:

Tuesday 23 August 1768
*'I saw a serious congregation at Taunton!
And shall we have fruit here also? In the
evening I preached to the poor backslid-
ers at Cullompton.'*

He was influential in the establishment
of the former Octagon Chapel in Middle
Street which was opened in 1776. In fact,
the deeds defined the use of the building
to '....The Rev. John Wesley......and such
other persons as he should from time to
time appoint that they may therein preach
and expound God's holy word.'
  He preached at the Octagon 13 times be-
tween 1776 and 1789, the last time when he was 86. This time he was able to
report:

*'In the evening we had such a congregation as, I suppose, was never in that
house before.'*

He died two years later.

Whitmash Family

By 1690 John Whitmash was offering a weekly service to The Bell Inn in
Wood Street, London. The main goods that were transported were serge (woollen cloth). He was unlikely to have been the first carrier to London but he is
the first for which we have any detailed knowledge. The journey at this time
would probably have taken close to a full week and would have been by wagon.
When his son, also called John, inherited the business after his death in 1724,
he added Stage Coaches to the wagon service and expanded into Yeovil. Over
the years the journey times for coaches decreased in part due to longer hours on
the road and earlier starts but later on with improvements to the road surfaces
and the introduction of steel springs into the carriages. By 1730 the journey to
London was taking four days. By 1765, after the introduction of toll roads, its
was down to just two days.
 A third John Whitmash took over the carrying business after the second John
Whitmash died in January 1769, though in September 1769 he sold it to William Cockerham and Thomas Liley of Yeovil. It changed hands several times

in the years between 1769 and 1841 including a spell of six years with John Whitmash III as owner and, later, Henry Whitmash his younger brother. Both eventually formed an association with partners outside the family. Much of the traffic was generated from Yeovil which had prospered as Taunton's trade in serge declined (though it was in part replaced by silk).

The Whitmash family kept faith with their coach interests. Their main routes were to London, Barnstaple, Exeter and Bath and Bristol. By 1827 the journey time from Taunton to London was down to 19 hours with average speeds increasing from 4.6 m.p.h. to 8.7 m.p.h. The number of coach services increased dramatically between 1730 and 1830. In 1730 there was only one service per week to London, Exeter and Bristol. By 1830 there were six coaches a week to London, 13 to Barnstaple, 28 to Exeter and 29 to Bristol and Bath. The Velocity introduced in 1834, 'a new splendid and rapid conveyance', cut down the time even further.

In the beginning the rise of the railway was not all bad for the coach industry as it gave a stimulus to short coach journeys to and from the railway sta-

tions. However, as the network was extended, first to Bridgwater in June 1841, to Taunton in July 1842 and Exeter in May 1844, the firms days became numbered and by 1848 it had ceased to exist.

SANHS

Wool

The woollen industry dates back to the 13th century when there was a fulling mill in Taunton where the wool was cleaned and thickened. By the 15th century cloth was being exported to France via the port at Lyme Regis. In the late 16th century a higher quality 'Spanish' cloth began to be manufactured and by the 17th century became the most important wool product made in Taunton. Taunton dominated the wool trade in Somerset and a yarn market had become established by the end of the 1620's. However, with the outbreak of war with Spain in 1655 and the growth of a rival Irish cloth industry, the cloth industry in Taunton began to decline. Serge, which had been popular, began to go out of fashion. In 1681 there were believed to be 500 unemployed serge workers. The situation was excacerbated by the war with France in 1687. There was a ban on foreign exports from Ireland in 1699 and there was a brief revival of the trade in

Taunton at the beginning of the 18th century. In the second quarter of the 18th century, though, with changes in fashion, increased competition from more efficient spinning machines introduced in the North, and possibly, the disruption caused by contested elections, the trade saw a serious decline. However, a new industry, silk weaving was introduced into the town in the 1770's.

Workhouse

The Bridewell situated on the Tone Bridge had been an early type of workhouse thought to have been built in the last quarter of the 16th century and linked to another workhouse in Staplegrove. Over the years the Bridewell began to be used more as a prison.

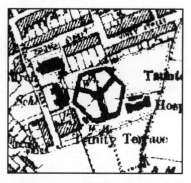

A parliamentary report put together during 1776-7 showed work houses operating in Taunton St James (for up to 40 inmates), Taunton St Mary Magdalene (up to 80 inmates), Bishop's Hull (up to 22 inmates), Lydeard St Lawrence (up to 16 inmates) and North Curry (up to 20 inmates).

The heaxagonal workhouse as shown on an 1889 edition of a 1:10560 map (not to scale)

Following the implementation of the 1834 Poor Law Amendment Act, the Taunton Poor Law Union came into existence on 12 May 1836. In keeping with the new act it introduced a centrally administered system which centred on the workhouse. The Taunton Union Workhouse, based on a design by the young architect, Sampson Kempthorne, was built at Trinity Street between 1836 and 1838 covering a total population of 31,378. The population of the town at this time was a little over 11,000. Kempthorne was paid £3.50 for each £100 spent on building the workhouse. The design was amended so that two fire-places rather then one were installed in the boardroom and the number of toilets per ward was reduced from two to one. The workhouse was ready for opening in September 1838.

An outbreak of cholera had swept through the country and, until the autumn of 1849, Taunton had remained free of an outbreak. In fact, it was even contemplated that Queen Victoria should be evacuated to the convent at Taunton. However, there was an outbreak in the workhouse in November 1849. Within 24 hours 43 cases had been discovered. It was popularly believed, as stated in the Taunton Courier, that 'the disease was brought in by Catherine Hurley, a female tramp from Bridgwater.' This had been the conclusion of the medical officer, a Mr Foster, who had conducted the post-mortem on her without the permission of the Board of Guardians. She was later found not to have had cholera. Dr Foster had asked, however, for the diet to be improved when he was appointed in March 1849. This was not implemented until after a damming report on the cholera epidemic by Dr Sutherland from the Ministry of Health in London.

Panic ensued, with the guardians meeting twice a day while the epidemic lasted. Reports were heard of inmates who had been taken ill and those who had died. A slightly bizarre aspect was the positioning of a guard outside each WC to report anyone using it more than once a day. Those that did were given 'a purge of rice water'. Within three weeks 59 had died including the schoolmaster.

As well as complaining about the defective diet, Dr Sutherland criticised the amount of space given to each person in the workhouse and the low ceilings, 'much too low to admit a proper circulation of air in them', the general arrangement and positioning of the toilets, 'not the ones best adapted to ensure the purity of the atmosphere while in the ward set apart for the cholera cases the water closet forms in reality part of the ward.' The guardians denied they were in any way responsible. On his second visit on the 10 November he was disappointed that many of his recommendations had not yet been implemented and that many of the inmates remained in the work house.

The children were evacuated from the workhouse to a room at Trinity School by permission of the Rev. F. J. Smith on the understanding that they would be returned to the workhouse if they became ill. By the 12 November arrangements were made for the evacuation of adult evacuees to Orchard Portman and, despite many protests from parishioners, this was followed by an evacuation to Fyfet House at Otterford. Remarkably, the outbreak was contained and nobody died from cholera outside the workhouse.

After the cholera epidemic, a second building was erected as a hospital and some of the school buildings were improved. These enhancements were completed in 1851.

There was also an epidemic of smallpox in 1871), scarletina in 1874 and measles in 1878.

In 1838, a Mr Willment was appointed the master of the workhouse and his wife the nurse. On 10 June 1840 Mr Willment was charged with 'being seen on a Sunday with Charlotte W., one of the inmates of the Workhouse, on his knees in the nurses room.' He was brought before the Board of Guardians and two inmates were questioned in his presence. Though he denied the charge, he was found guilty and given a warning.

The schoolmaster and schoolmistress were also an important part of the workhouse set-up. Robert Hodder, who was the first appointed, along with his wife, Heziah, was called before the Board of Guardians for punishing a three year old child 'too severely'. Punishments thereafter had to be witnessed by the Master or the Matron. He was later reported to have 'misconducted himself towards one of the female paupers.' There were no witnesses so the complaint was dismissed.

There was a rapid turnover of nurses, especially after the cholera epidemic of 1849. In 1874, a Nurse Orme resigned. In her letter to the local government board she complained about the lack of brandy given to the inmates. Alcohol was regularly used as a reward within the workhouse, though it should be said that it was very often in the form of a weak beer drunk in preference to the

Part of the workhose whcih still remains, now converted into flats

water. In 1878, the quota for women working in the laundry, two wardsmen, two paupers, two gardeners and the cook and a kitchen woman was two pints daily. The woman who cared for the infants was allowed one pint.

The other important appointments were the medical officer and the Chaplain. The first medical officer was appointed in 1837 on £50 a year. The Chaplain could be influential. Following the complaint of the Chaplain to the Board of Guardians in 1875, the master was sacked.

The 1881 census shows 198 residents in the workhouse ranging from the ages of 1-93. In some cases whole families were institutionalised, the largest of these being the Yard family comprising Alice (1), John (2), Joseph (4), Mary Anne (5), Charlotte (8), Jane (10), Clara (11), Ann (13) and the mother, Elizabeth (36). No father is mentioned.

The most hated occupation was 'bone-crushing', the crushing of animal bones to make bone-meal fertiliser. This was eventually outlawed. Other occupations included stone-breaking, chopping wood, gardening and household chores. As an alternative to stone-breaking women could pick oakum. This involved the unpicking of a tarred rope for recycling.

Vagrants were also allowed to sleep in the workhouse as long as they worked for their keep. In 1867, for example, a man was required to break 2 cwts of rock and a woman to pick 3 lbs of oakum.

Boys and girls including brothers and sisters were completely segregated.

Before the building of the county asylum in Wells in 1848, the medical officer had the option of putting lunatics in the workhouse. Alternatives were to give 'out relief', where the case was not too severe or where supervision was available, say from a relative. Where the case was severe, or for example, the subject was considered violent, they would be sent to Fairwater House (now part of Taunton School), though at 12s a week this was generally considered too expensive an option. They were later sent to Dr Langworthy of Kingsdown and Box at 8s a head.

Yea, Sir William

The owner of Pyrland Hall. A gang led by Thomas Gage broke into the house and tied up Sir William. He managed to escape by cutting himself free with a carving knife and the thieves left without saying anything. Gage was executed at Dodhill Green nearby. At the moment of execution Sir William told the hangman to 'turn the rascal round and let the people see him.'

Young, Arthur (1741 - 1820)

After experimenting with new farming methods as a manager on a farm he spent most of his life travelling in England, Wales, Ireland and France arguing for agricultural improvement. He wrote the Annals of Agriculture in 45 volumes between 1784 and 1809. The following extract is from 1776: Tour of South Wales and South Midlands.

'They do fame about Taunton in Somersetshire, and a very good way it is, the tramps yield more food than the weeds do stubble, and the land gets an autumnal ploughing. Wheat yields from 2 to 3 qrs. Barley, 4 to 5. Oats 5 to 6. This, however, is not a universal system, for they do not sow more turnips than they can fold; in their turnip fallow, they destroy the couch by harrowing, then raking it in heaps and burning it: The farm-yard dung, caleed here pot-dung, is all laid on for wheat; a great blunder, it ought all to go to turnips. They know very well the value of sainforne, sowing many fields with it. It lasts fifteen years, and yields two tons of hay per acre, worth 45s. a ton. Soot is the favourable manure for it; lay ten bushels an acre, at 4d but think they breed couch. This is a circumstance, which deserves attention: any manure being apt to bring weeds, is only a proof of its excellence, though usually condemned by its farmers, for that quality. Their soils are very dry; now I have on many occasions remarked, that from the wet land these ashes are useless, but yield a great effect on good dry loams.

The flock in this country are large: and ewes for breeding, the profit being the lamb and the wool; they fold the year through; but at lambing in the farm-yard.

In stocking the farms, they reckon 200l. necessary for one of 500l. a year.

Price of labour, 1s. a day till harvest, then 10s. a week, for 6 weeks.

Youngest Inherits

The laws of succession within the tenure of the manor Taunton Deane were unusual in that the normal laws of primogeniture where the eldest son would inherit were reversed. The fifteenth article states, 'if he (the tenant) hath more sons than one, the youngest son hath used to hath and inherit the same, as sole heir to his father, by the custom of the said manor.' The same principle applies where there is more than one daughter and no sons, so that 'the youngest daughter ought and have used to inherit the same, as sole heir to her said father.'

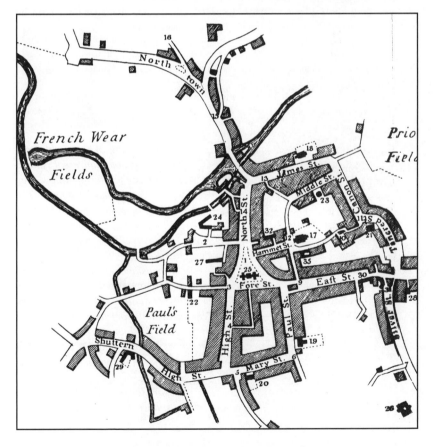

Map of Taunton about 1790. Not to scale

Taunton: An A - Z

Taunton Timeline

3500 BC. Evidence of Bronze Age Occupation at Norton Hill Fort near Taunton.

722 The destruction of a settlement in Taunton founded by King Ina is recorded in the Anglo-Saxon Chronicles.

904 First charter granted by King Edward the Elder.

10th century A mint is established in Taunton. Coins are made here well into the 12th century.

c1120 First Priory is built in Taunton and the first prior, Guy of Merton is appointed.

1136 First borough charter granted by King Stephen.

1138 A Keep is built by the Bishop of Winchester, Henry de Blois, in the grounds of the current Castle Hotel.

1158 Priory moves to a new site east of the Castle.

1162 St Mary Magdalene and St James's Church were both established by this time.

c1208 Two ponds or vivaria established on the south side of the town.

1290 Humphrey Kael and William de Staunton are chosen as the first MP's for Taunton.

1389 The Archdeacon Of Taunton, Piero Tomacelli becomes Pope Boniface IX.

1451 A skirmish in the Wars of the Roses between Lord Bonville (Lancastrian) and Thomas de Courtney (Yorkist).

1488 Mary Magdalene church tower is begun (completed 1514).

1497 The Provost of Penrhyn, a hated tax-collector is chased into Taunton by irate Cornishmen and hacked to pieces in the Market Square.

In September Perkin Warbeck, pretender to the King, comes to Taunton with 8,000 men but flees and is then captured and brought back to Taunton Castle.

1522 Grammar School is opened in the Old Municipal Building at the instigation of Bishop Fox.

1529 Thomas Cromwell made MP for Taunton.

1530 Thomas Cranmer appointed Archdeacon of Taunton.

1539 The Priory is closed by Henry VIII

1627 Taunton granted a new charter. First Mayor, Andrew Healey, is appointed.

1635 Gray's Almshouses established.

1642 In August the Civil War begins and Taunton declares itself for Parliament.

1643 In June Taunton is taken over by Royalist forces.

1644 Taunton is taken by a Parliamentarian army led by Robert Blake.

1645 On the 11 May the Royalist troops end their long siege of Taunton and retreat to Bridgwater.

1660 Charles II removes Taunton's charter and orders the destruction of Taunton Castle.

1668 Joseph Alleine dies.

c1672 First congregation at Paul's Meeting House.

1677 Taunton is granted a new charter, but the officers are hand-picked and required to take the oath of allegiance.

Taunton: An A - Z

1682 A Market House is built.

1685 The Duke of Monmouth is crowned King in Taunton but defeated at Sedgemoor. Over 150 are hung following the Bloody Assizes presided over by Judge Jeffreys.

1688 Taunton's charter is renewed by James II, but it is even more biased towards the crown.

The Glorious Revolution heralding the reign of William and Mary is welcomed in Taunton.

1698 Celia Fiennes visits Taunton.

1716 First printing press is established in Taunton.

c1721 Mary Street Chapel is built.

1725 On 21 May the first edition of the Taunton Journal is printed.

1752 Turnpike Act for Taunton.

1756 Wilton Gaol opened.

1770 The last market cross, High Cross, is removed.

1772 A new Market House completed by Copplestone Warre Bampfylde.

c1778 Silk manufacturing introduced to the town.

1786 First theatre is opened by James Biggs in East Reach.

1788 Hammett Street is built.

Racing takes place at Broomfield.

1791 Joshua Toulmin publishes the first history of Taunton.

1792 The Taunton charter lapses.

1794 William Marshall visits Taunton and describes it as 'the Golden Vale'.

1797 United Reformed Church is built.

1800 A theatre opened in Silver Street.

1807 The Crescent is built.

1808 Temple Methodist Chapel begun.

1812 First hospital built in East Reach.

1815 Wilton gaol extended.

1816 Eye Infirmary established.

Billett Street built (by James Billett).

c1821 Gas lighting introduced.

Another market house, The New Market House completed in Fore Street.

1823 Bridgwater and Taunton Canal is begun.

1829 Joseph Sewell, the blind giant dies.

1835 Disraeli contests and loses an election in Taunton.

1838 Taunton Workhouse opened.

1840 Police station built at Magdalene Lane.

1842 Railway reaches Taunton.

Holy Trinity Church built.

1843 Queens College established as the Wesleyan Proprietary Grammar School.

The County Court moves from Ilchester to Taunton.

1844 First publication of Eothen by Taunton born Alexander Kinglake.

North Street Chapel is opened.

1847 Taunton School is founded as the West of England Dissenters Proprietary School.

1848 Taunton adopts GMT and moves clocks forward 12 minutes.

1849 Somerset Archaeological and Natural History Society established.

1851 Taunton Cabinet exhibited at the Great Exhibition.

1853 Corn Exchange built next to Castle Bow.

1856 New police station built at the junction of the Crescent and Upper High Street.

1858 Piped water introduced.

Shire Hall opened.

1860 St George's Church opened.

1862 The West Somerset Railway from Taunton to Watchet is completed.

1863 St John the Evangelist Church is opened.

1866 School of Art is established in Bath Place.

The Bridgwater and Taunton Canal is sold to the Exeter railway Company.

1871 Devon & Somerset Railway opened from Norton Fitzwarren to Wiveliscombe.

1872 The Urban Sanitary Authority is formed.

1873 Devon & Somerset Railway is extended to Barnstaple (Closed in 1966).

1874 The West Somerset Railway is extended to Minehead.

Somerset Archaeological and Natural History Society buy the Castle to house a museum.

1875 Somerset County Cricket Club Founded.

1877 Taunton is granted its final charter.

1879 On 13 January first exhibition of electric lights in front of the Victoria Rooms on the Parade.

1880 Jellalabad Barracks built.

Canon Woodard opens Kings Alfred's College (now King's College).

1881 St Andrew's Church is built.

1883 Edward Goldsworthy publishes his pamphlet of reminiscences.

1885 Taunton now sends one MP to parliament rather than two.

1890 Railway accident at Norton Fitzwarren.

1894 Corporation Street is opened.

1895 Vivary Park laid out.

1897 Tone Vale Hospital opened (Closed in 1991).

1898 The first Taunton amateur opera, In the Days of the Siege, is performed at the London Hotel Assembly Rooms.

1901 First trams run in Taunton.

1903 Buffalo Bill comes to Taunton.

1904 Tom Locke, the last Potwalloper dies.

1905 Library opens in Corporation Street.

Bishop Fox's School moves to Staplegrove Road.

1907 School of Art opens in Corporation Street.

1910 Picturedrome (later The Exchange Theatre) and the County Cinema begin showing silent films.

1911 The Post Office is opened in North Street.

1921 Taunton Cider established as a limited company.

1922 Priory Bridge opens as the tram system closes.

1927 Racecourse built.

1928 Between 26 and 30 July a Grand Pageant entitled Defendamus takes place.

1929 The market moves to Priory Bridge Road.

1934 A new Coat of Arms is adopted by the College of Arms.

1935 Taunton replaces Weston-Super-Mare as the County Town.

1937 The Corn Exchange building is demolished and replaced by a new building to house the electricity board showroom.

1939 Large numbers are evacuated to Taunton.

1940 A second serious rail crash at Norton Fitzwarren.

Bishop Fox's School moves to Kingston Road from Staplegrove Road.

1941 Printing of Hydrographic charts begun in Taunton.

1947 The Bridgwater and Taunton Canal is taken over by the British Waterways Board.

1951 Musgrove Hospital established as part of the NHS.

1955 Lisieux becomes a twin town.

1959 St Teresa's Church, Eastwick Road

Somerset College of Art and Technology established at Wellington Road.

1960 Severe flooding in Taunton.

1964 Richard Huish Grammar School moves to South Road.

1968 Severe flooding

Hydrographic Office moves to an integrated site at Taunton.

1974 The Borough of Taunton becomes Taunton Deane Borough Council.

M5 Motorway comes to Taunton (Junction 25).

1977 Brewhouse Theatre opens.

1979 Richard Huish Sixth Form College Established.

1982 Old Market shopping Centre is opened.

1985 County Walk Opens.

1987 Queen visits on the 4 May.

1984 Taunton is twinned with Koenigslutter in Lower Saxony.

1994 Bishop Fox's moves to Calway Road.

1995 The Hestercombe Gardens Project is begun.

Taunton Cider is sold to Matthew Clarke.

1997 For the first time the public are excluded from the flower show due to a freak flash flood.

2000 Severe flooding.

Hestercombe Gardens Trust established

2005 Silk Mills Bridge opens

2007 Somerset County Cricket Club are promoted to the first division of the County Championship and the Pro40 League.

2008 Taunton wins National Britain in Bloom title for the first time.

Taunton: An A - Z

Bibliography

Abdy, R & Brunning, R. A. & Webster, C. J., Journal of Archaeology 14, The Discovery of a Roman Villa & its Severan Coin Hoard of 9238 Silver Denarii.

Alleine, Joseph, An Alarm to the Unconverted (1672)

Baker, Gordon, The History of Huish's Taunton (1980).

Bentley, J. B. & Murless, B.J., The Legacy of the Turnpike Trusts.

Berry, Rosemary, The History of the Convent in Taunton.

Bland, Roger & Burnett, Andrew, The Normanby Coin Hoard & Other Hoards

Bromwich, David, King's College, Taunton.

Brooke, L.E.J. Various unpublished collections in the Somerset Studies Library.

Brown, John, Independent Witness. (1997)

Bumber, Michael, Robert Blake, Oxford Dictionary of National Biography (2004).

Bush, Robin, Jeboult's Taunton (1983).

Bush, Robin, The County Hotel.

Bush, Robin, The Book of Taunton (1977)

Bush, Robin, Taunton Castle: a Pictorial History (1988).

Bush, Kettlewell & Wilkie, Taunton Amateur Operatic Society.

Cambden, William, Brittania (1607), translated by Philemon Holland.

Castle Hotel booklet

Chambers Biographical Dictionary (1990).

Chanon, H. J., The History of Queen's College.

Cousin, John William, A Short Biographical Dictionary of English Literature. (1910).

Defoe, Daniel, A Tour Through the Whole Island of Britain (1978)

Dorchester, Sherborne & Taunton Journal.

Dunning, Robert), (ed), Somerset Churches & Chapels: Building, Repair and Restoration.

Encyclopedia Brittanica,1911 edition.

Fiennes, Celia, Through England on a Side Saddle.

Forbes, Archibald, The Afghan Wars.

Friends Meeting House, Taunton, Quakers in Taunton

Gathercole, Clare, An Archaeological Assessment of Taunton (2002).

.Gerard, Thomas, Survey of West Somersetshire.

Gerhold, Dorian, Whitmash Family. Proceedings vol. 143 (1999)

Gledhill, David & Lamb, Peter, Electricity in Taunton 1809-1948.

Goldsworthy, Edward, Recollections of Old Taunton (1992).

Goodman's Taunton Guides and Directory 1864,1887-8, 1902 -3.

Grant, Liz, The Somerset Light Infantry, 1685-1968.

Guardian Newspaper, 12 January 2007. Obituary Column: Mandy.

Guy, John, Tudor England, 1990.

Hawkins, Mac, Somerset at War.

Hestercombe Gardens Booklet.

Haskell, Tony, The Bridgwater & Taunton Canal (2007).

Holder, Robert, Taunton Cider and The Langdons. (2000).

Hugo, Thomas, The History of Taunton Priory.

Jenner, The Monmouth Rebellion and the Battle of Sedgemoor.

Johns, Nigel, Somerset County Cricket Club, First Class Records.
Johnson, Ruth, 100 Years of Norton Fitzwarren.
Jones, M. H., Harry Frier's Taunton (2002).
Keegan, John, Whose Who in Military History (1996).
Kelly's Directory of Somerset, 1895.
Kingdom, A. R., Railway Accident at Norton Fitzwarren.
Kinglake, Alexander, Eothen.
Kirk, Revd Brian, The Taunton Dissenting Academy (1988).
Lawrence, Eddie, Somerset County Cricket Club: 100 Greats.
Marshall, William, The Rural Economy of the West of England.
Mason, Simon, The History of Bishop Fox's School
Mathew, H, et al, Oxford Dictionary of National Biography (2004)
Mayberry, Tom, The Vale of Taunton Past (1998).
Minnit, Durnell & Gunstone, Somerset Public House Tokens (1985).
Morris, John (ed), The Domesday Book: Somerset, Phillimore (1980).
Morris, Admiral, History of the UK Hydrographic Office in Peace and War.
The National Archives
Pedler, Garth, A Prep School in Somerset.
Perkin, John, Taunton Trams.
Perkin, John, Arc Lighting in Taunton 1879-1910.
Pigot's Directory of Somerset, 1822 & 1830.
Pollock, John: The Man Behind the Legend (1993).
Porter, John, Crosse Connections: a 19th Century Scientist and his Family (2006).
Queen's College Taunton Prospectus.
Record, S. P., Proud Century (1948).
Ritchie, G.S., The Admiralty Chart.
Robson's Directory of Somerset, 1839.
Russell, William Howard, The British Expedition to the Crimea (1858).
Scott, Paul, Remembering Those Passing Flickering Shadows (1998)
Seventh Report of the Inspector of Prisons: Wilton Gaol.
Somerset and Dorset Notes and Queries.
Somerset County Gazette.
Somerset County Herald.
Stanier, Peter, Somerset in the Age of Steam (2003).
Stedall, Tony, Somerset County Cricket Club.
Sweetman, John, The Crimean War (2001).
Symmonds, Henry, Taunton Tokens of the 17th Century. Proceedings 1911 SANHS
The Taunton Journal
Toulmin, Joshua, History of Taunton (Savage edition, 1822)
Trevilian, M. F. Cely, & Tanner, E. Laurence, Defendamus: a Pageant of Taunton.
Victoria County History Vol. II.
Wesley, John, Journal.
Wilson, Jeffrey, The Somerset Home Guard (2004)
Wroughton, John, An Unhappy Civil War.